First World War
and Army of Occupation
War Diary
France, Belgium and Germany

1 DIVISION
1 Infantry Brigade
Loyal North Lancashire Regiment
1st Battalion
1 February 1918 - 16 April 1919

WO95/1266/1

The Naval & Military Press Ltd
www.nmarchive.com
Published in association with The National Archives

Published by

The Naval & Military Press Ltd

Unit 10 Ridgewood Industrial Park,

Uckfield, East Sussex,

TN22 5QE England

Tel: +44 (0) 1825 749494

www.naval-military-press.com

www.nmarchive.com

This diary has been reprinted in facsimile from the original. Any imperfections are inevitably reproduced and the quality may fall short of modern type and cartographic standards.

© **Crown Copyright**
Images reproduced by permission of The National Archives, London, England, 2015.

Contents

Document type	Place/Title	Date From	Date To
Heading	WO95/1266/1		
Heading	1st Division 1st Infy Bde 1st Battalion Loyal Nth Lancs Regt. Feb-Dec 1918 From 2 Bde 1 Div		
War Diary	Reninghof Farm	01/02/1918	09/02/1918
War Diary	California Dug-Outs	09/02/1918	23/02/1918
War Diary	Hugel Halles (Support Area)	24/02/1918	24/02/1918
War Diary	Norfolk House	15/02/1918	02/03/1918
War Diary	Hugel Halles	03/03/1918	04/03/1918
War Diary	Siege Camp	05/03/1918	09/03/1918
War Diary	Souvenir House	09/03/1918	13/03/1918
War Diary	Huddleston Camp	13/03/1918	17/03/1918
War Diary	Kempton Park	17/03/1918	21/03/1918
War Diary	Souvenir House	22/03/1918	25/03/1918
War Diary	Canal Bank	26/03/1918	29/03/1918
War Diary	Caine Trench	30/03/1918	31/03/1918
Operation(al) Order(s)	1st Loyal North Lancs Regiment Order No. 89	24/03/1918	24/03/1918
Miscellaneous	Appendix "A"		
Miscellaneous	Appendix "B"		
Miscellaneous	Report On Raid Carried Out By "B" Company 1st Battalion Loyal North Lancashire Regiment In The Early Morning Of March 25th 1918	25/03/1918	25/03/1918
Map	Map		
Heading	1st Brigade 1st Division 1st Battalion Loyal North Lancashire Regiment April 1918		
War Diary	Cane Trench	01/04/1918	02/04/1918
War Diary	In The Line Souvenir Farm U.18.c.3.6.	03/04/1918	08/04/1918
War Diary	Lapugnoy	09/04/1918	10/04/1918
War Diary	Houchin	11/04/1918	11/04/1918
War Diary	Beuvry	12/04/1918	15/04/1918
War Diary	Le Preol	15/04/1918	15/04/1918
War Diary	In The Line	16/04/1918	23/04/1918
War Diary	Houchin	24/04/1918	24/04/1918
War Diary	Neoux Les Mines	25/04/1918	30/04/1918
Miscellaneous	1st Bn L N Lancs Rt Operations Orders-Night of 6/7th April	06/04/1918	06/04/1918
Miscellaneous	Operations Orders	17/09/1918	17/09/1918
Miscellaneous	Headquarters 1st Infantry Brigade Report on Fighting Patrols Carries Out on The Night 6/7th April	07/04/1918	07/04/1918
War Diary	Noeux Les Mines	01/05/1918	27/05/1918
War Diary	In The Line	28/05/1918	31/05/1918
Miscellaneous	Extracts from Battalion Orders 1st Battalion Loyal North Lancashire Regiment	22/05/1918	22/05/1918
War Diary	Hohenzollern Sector	01/06/1918	01/06/1918
War Diary	Annequin	02/06/1918	04/06/1918
War Diary	Hohenzollern Sector	05/06/1918	20/06/1918
War Diary	Neoux-Les-Mines	21/06/1918	21/06/1918
War Diary	Cambrin	22/06/1918	24/06/1918
War Diary	In The Line	25/06/1918	03/07/1918
War Diary	Cambrin	04/07/1918	11/07/1918
War Diary	Noeux Les Mines	10/07/1918	20/07/1918

War Diary	Annequin		21/07/1918	26/07/1918
War Diary	In The Field		27/07/1918	10/08/1918
War Diary	Noeux Les Mines		11/08/1918	12/08/1918
War Diary	Camp K 23 C & D		13/08/1918	18/08/1918
War Diary	Predefin		19/08/1918	31/08/1918
War Diary	Arras		01/09/1918	02/09/1918
War Diary	Drocourt Queant Line		03/09/1918	07/09/1918
War Diary	Y Huts W of Arras		08/09/1918	10/09/1918
War Diary	Morcourt		11/09/1918	12/09/1918
War Diary	Estrees		13/09/1918	13/09/1918
War Diary	Poeilly		14/09/1918	14/09/1918
War Diary	Vermand		15/09/1918	15/09/1918
War Diary	In The Line		16/09/1918	03/10/1918
War Diary	South Of Lehaucourt		04/10/1918	04/10/1918
War Diary	Vermand		05/10/1918	08/10/1918
War Diary	N W of Bellenglise		09/10/1918	15/10/1918
War Diary	Bohain		16/10/1918	16/10/1918
War Diary	S E Of Becquigny		17/10/1918	18/10/1918
War Diary	La Vallee Mulatre		19/10/1918	20/10/1918
War Diary	Wassigny		23/10/1918	30/10/1918
Miscellaneous	Headquarters 1st Brigade Reference Maps 62c SE And 62b Am S.W. 1/20000		06/10/1918	06/10/1918
Miscellaneous	Narrative of Operations of 1st Division on September 18th And 19th 1918			
Map	Map			
Miscellaneous	The Recipient Is Responsible That The Instructions Contained In D.R.O. No 936		21/10/1918	21/10/1918
Miscellaneous	Narrative of Operations of 1st Division on 24th September 1918		24/09/1918	24/09/1918
Map	Map			
Miscellaneous	Narrative of Operations of 1st Division 29th September To 3rd October 1918		03/10/1918	03/10/1918
Map	Map			
Miscellaneous	Officer Commanding 1st Loyal North Lancs. Regt.		07/10/1918	07/10/1918
Miscellaneous	Report On Operations 26th September To 4th October 1918		07/10/1918	07/10/1918
Miscellaneous	Report On Part Taken By The 1st Battalion Loyal North Lancashire Regiment		17/10/1918	17/10/1918
War Diary	Wassigny		01/11/1918	03/11/1918
War Diary	Ribeauville		05/11/1918	05/11/1918
War Diary	Molain		06/11/1918	06/11/1918
War Diary	Fresnoy Le Grand		07/11/1918	11/11/1918
War Diary	Grand Fayt		13/11/1918	14/11/1918
War Diary	Sars Poteries		15/11/1918	15/11/1918
War Diary	Hestrud		16/11/1918	17/11/1918
War Diary	Boussu-Lez-Walcourt		18/11/1918	18/11/1918
War Diary	Fraire		19/11/1918	22/11/1918
War Diary	Flavion		24/11/1918	24/11/1918
War Diary	Chateau Melin Onhaye		25/11/1918	28/11/1918
War Diary	Chateau Melin		28/11/1918	30/11/1918
Miscellaneous	Narrative of Operations of 1st Division 4th November 1918		08/11/1918	08/11/1918
Miscellaneous	WO95/1266			
Map	Map			
Map	Barzy			
Map	Map			

Miscellaneous	Lieut Col. R.E. Berkeley D.S.O. Comdg 1st L.North Lancs Regt.	07/11/1918	07/11/1918
War Diary	Near Onhaye	01/12/1918	01/12/1918
War Diary	Celles	02/12/1918	02/12/1918
War Diary	Chevetogne	03/12/1918	09/12/1918
War Diary	Baillonville	10/12/1918	10/12/1918
War Diary	Barvaux	11/12/1918	11/12/1918
War Diary	Mormont	12/12/1918	13/12/1918
War Diary	Odeigne	14/12/1918	14/12/1918
War Diary	Les Sart	15/12/1918	15/12/1918
War Diary	Courtil	16/12/1918	16/12/1918
War Diary	Krombach	17/12/1918	17/12/1918
War Diary	Manderfeld	18/12/1918	18/12/1918
War Diary	Dahlem	19/12/1918	19/12/1918
War Diary	Blankenheimerdorf	20/12/1918	21/12/1918
War Diary	Munstereifel	22/12/1918	22/12/1918
War Diary	Kluckenheim	23/12/1918	23/12/1918
Heading	1st Division 1st Infy Bde 1st Bn Loyal Nth Lancs Jan-Apr 1919		
War Diary	Bornheim	01/01/1919	31/01/1919
Miscellaneous	1st Brigade No. G. 1/415	09/01/1919	09/01/1919
Miscellaneous	Narrative of Operations of 1st Division on October 17th 18th & 19th 1918	19/10/1918	19/10/1918
War Diary	Bornheim	01/02/1919	31/03/1919
Miscellaneous	D.A.G. G.H.Q. 3rd Echelon	22/04/1919	22/04/1919
War Diary	Bornheim	01/04/1919	14/04/1919
War Diary	Dunkirk	15/04/1919	16/04/1919

WO 95/1266/1

1ST DIVISION
1ST INFY BDE

1ST BATTALION
LOYAL NTH LANCS REGT.
FEB - DEC 1918

FROM 2 BDE 1 DIV

Army Form C. 2118.

Came from 2nd Bn 7.2.18.

WAR DIARY

1st Battalion The Loyal North Lancashire Regiment

February 1918

INTELLIGENCE SUMMARY

(Erase heading not required.)

Instructions regarding War Diaries and Intelligence Summaries are contained in F. S. Regs., Part II. and the Staff Manual respectively. Title pages will be prepared in manuscript.

Place	Date	Hour	Summary of Events and Information	Remarks and references to Appendices
REVINGHOF FARM	1.2/18 to 4.2/18		Training. Range firing. Gas Chamber and Rifle Bombing. Platoon and Company training. Several small Musketry Contests were held.	
	5.2/18		After nearly 4 years service together, the Battalion was transferred from the 2nd Brigade; consequent upon the reorganisation of Brigades into 3 Battalion instead of 4. The record of 4 years continuous service in a Brigade, 3½ years at least of which in the other Brigade could boast, and consequently the feeling, although mainly changing Brigades was rather a wrench.	
	6.2/18 to 8.2/18		Training continued, though for the last few days it was largely interfered with by weather conditions. 2/Lt G.W.P. HOWART + 2/Lt H.P. CRANE joined 6/2.	
	9.2/18		The Division moved down and took over the PINEAPPLE Section from 35th Division with 1 Brigade (2nd) in the line, 1 Brigade (1st) in Support, and 1 Brigade (3rd) in Reserve. The Battalion relieved the 12th D.L.I. in the Support area in CALIFORNIA DUG-OUTS (C.22.C.59) slightly North of WIELTJE. Unfortunately the enemy took it into his head to shell this area just before + just after the Battalion arrived & the first casualties they sustained 3 of own advanced party, and on the second	

Army Form C. 2118.

WAR DIARY
or
INTELLIGENCE SUMMARY.
(Erase heading not required.)

Instructions regarding War Diaries and Intelligence Summaries are contained in F. S. Regs., Part II. and the Staff Manual respectively. Title pages will be prepared in manuscript.

Place	Date	Hour	Summary of Events and Information	Remarks and references to Appendices
CALIFORNIA DUG-OUTS.	9.2.18		Germans unfortunately hit our dug out caused 10 casualties 1 killed and 9 wounded of whom 2 subsequently died. 2nd Lt. J. Midgely rejoined the Battalion today	
	10.2.18 to 19.2.18		Quiet days. Battalion engaged on works on Army Line. Draft of 160 O.R. joined. Last detachment of 200 posted from 7th Royal Irish Regt.	
	20.2.18 to "		Battalion moved up at Dusk and relieved 1/5th Northampton in Right Forward Section of the Division's front, from V.28.A.3.4. to V.20.D.6.6. Dispositions:—	
	22.2.18		Right Front Company C Coy. Centre Company A Coy. — both Coy HQ at Burn's House. Left Company B Coy with HQ at OXFORD HOUSE. Support D Coy South of WINCHESTER with 1 Platoon in TERRIER FARM. Battalion Head Quarters at HUBNER. On our right were 2 Northamptons. 8th Division and 12 Cameron on our left. During quiet tour of 2 days spent in this sector without incident or casualties. Relieved by 1st Black Watch on evening of March 14th & moved back into the Support area, 3 Companies along the ridge at MARINE VIEW and 2 in PHEASANT TRENCH with Battalion HQrs at HUGH HALLES.	
	23.2.18		Most of the day was spent in reconnaissance of left forward area. Some shelling during the day of both all Company areas but luckily no casualties were caused	

Army Form C. 2118.

WAR DIARY
or
INTELLIGENCE SUMMARY.
(Erase heading not required.)

Instructions regarding War Diaries and Intelligence Summaries are contained in F. S. Regs., Part II. and the Staff Manual respectively. Title pages will be prepared in manuscript.

Place	Date	Hour	Summary of Events and Information	Remarks and references to Appendices
HUGEL HALLES (Suffolk Sers)	24/2/18		Battalion moved out at dusk and took over the Left Sector of the Divisional Front from 1st Cameron Highlanders. Boundaries Y 20 D 66 to Y 14 A 41. Dispositions Right Front Company B, with HQ at GLOSTER FARM. Centre Coy A with HQ at PINEAPPLE Brewery. Left Front Coy D Coy, with HQ at FERDAN. Battalion Head Quarters at NORFOLK HOUSE.	hls hls hls hls
NORFOLK HOUSE	15/2/18 to 28/2/18		At first found little shelling of our area, what shelling occurred being mostly directed to back area. Desultory shelling - mainly expenditure - of MSUN/S B. Hillock resulted in several casualties 3 killed & 4 wounded. Relief immediately to other area went unmolested during its relief, but except in the area was quiet. Work was concentrated on the moving of the Outposts, to Main Line of Resistance, with good effects. The Battalion was due to be relieved by 1st Black Watch on the evening of Feb 28th, but owing to operations to be carried out by the Battalion in the Right Sector, the Battalion elected to remain in the line for 2 more days, to allow the 1st Cameron Highlanders to have a rest or rest on relief from the Right Sector, before moving into the left, and also to avoid the extra moves in returning to	hls hls hls hls hls hls hls hls hls hls

Army Form C. 2118.

WAR DIARY
or
INTELLIGENCE SUMMARY.
(Erase heading not required.)

Instructions regarding War Diaries and Intelligence Summaries are contained in F. S. Regs., Part II. and the Staff Manual respectively. Title pages will be prepared in manuscript.

Place	Date	Hour	Summary of Events and Information	Remarks and references to Appendices
NORFOLK HSE			Support area for 2 days and then returning to take over the line for 2 more. Lieut Bell joined from 7th O.S. attaln. Fighting strength of Battalion on 28th was :— 40 Officers 969 O.R.	Nil.

N.C. Phillips Lieut. Col.
Commdg. 1st Bn. Loyal N. Lancashire Regt.

N. Bouf Cox.
Bre Major MBoe.

SECRET

Army Form C. 2118.

WAR DIARY
or
INTELLIGENCE SUMMARY.
(Erase heading not required.)

1st Battalion The Loyal North Lancashire Regiment

March 1918

Instructions regarding War Diaries and Intelligence Summaries are contained in F.S. Regs., Part II. and the Staff Manual respectively. Title pages will be prepared in manuscript.

Place	Date	Hour	Summary of Events and Information	Remarks and references to Appendices
NORFOLK HOUSE.	1/3/18 to		Regt'l H'dqrs Belgium & France Sheet 28 B 14,000 & 7a.&.7b.a.e. BELGIUM. B.2. 1/10,000. A very quiet day. In the evening the 35th Division on our left carried out a raid, which brought down a certain amount of hostile retaliation on our front, but did not damage. Garrison of MEUNIER HOUSE was temporarily withdrawn to avoid casualties.	
" "	2/3/18		After another very quiet day, the Battalion was relieved by 1st Camerons and moved back into Support with our dispositions as before except that C & D Coys (formerly in PHEASANT TRENCH & MARINE VIEW respectively) changed over their positions.	※
HUGEL HALLES	3/3/18		A very quiet day. Battalion had a well deserved rest.	※
" "	4/3/18		3rd Bde relieved 1st Bde. Battalion was relieved by 12th S.W. Borders & moved back to BATTLE STATION, whence they entrained at READING STATION & moved into SIEGE CAMP No 6, about 1 mile South of ELVERDINGHE.	※
SIEGE CAMP	5/3/18 to 8/3/18		Resting, cleaning up and bathing. A warning order had already been issued that the Battalion might have to go up at short notice to relieve the Right Battalion of 35th Division on our left, and in our disaffection this move was ordered on 8th to take place the following day.	

(A7283) Wt. W8169/M1672 50,000 1/17 D D & L., London, E.C. Sch. 52a Forms/C/2118/4

Army Form C. 2118.

WAR DIARY
or
INTELLIGENCE SUMMARY.
(Erase heading not required.)

Instructions regarding War Diaries and Intelligence Summaries are contained in F. S. Regs., Part II. and the Staff Manual respectively. Title pages will be prepared in manuscript.

Place	Date	Hour	Summary of Events and Information	Remarks and references to Appendices
SIEGE CAMP	9/3/18		The Battalion moved up in the evening by train to BATTLE & thence by Motor Route to LANGEMARCK and the front area and relieved 12th HLI from the previous night. Nothern boundary of 1st Divisional Front Mt to YPRES-STADEN railway exclusive. Dispositions:— Right Front HCoy with 2 Platoons in East Outpost line around BOWER & BESACE (V.8.C.00) 1 Platoon at WATER HOUSE and 1 Platoon & Company HQ at MILLERS HOUSE. Left Front Coy. C. Coy with 2½ Platoons in Outpost line and 1½ Platoons and Coy HQ in TAUBE HOUSE. Support Company B Coy 3 Platoons less 1 Section at in shelters around V.13.C.4.2, 1 Section at SENEGAL, 1 Platoon at EAGLE TRENCH with Reserve Company. and Company HQ in OLGA HOUSES. Reserve A Coy in EAGLE TRENCH with Coy HQ at DOUBLE COTTS. Battalion HQs at SOUVENIR HOUSE. The relief was completed without any special incident, although the Boche offered to be engaged on area shoot, possibly owing to the amount of talking about the relief over the telephone which went on before the Battalion and been and then taken. On conclusion of relief, the Battalion came under the orders of G.O.C. 3rd Brigade, who was in charge of the whole Divisional Sector. Generally the method of holding the line as taken over was found to	

WAR DIARY
or
INTELLIGENCE SUMMARY.
(Erase heading not required.)

Army Form C. 2118.

Place	Date	Hour	Summary of Events and Information	Remarks and references to Appendices
SOUVENIR HOUSE	9/3/18 to 13/3/18		Enemy badly organised. Enemy MGs were found to be very active and direct fire onto the front posts of the Left Company and indirect fire upon our back areas, which caused us several casualties. Artillery fire was at no time heavy. A & B Coys were relieved by C & D Coys men respectively on the night of 11/12th. 1st CDSRs took over our Left Sector on evening of 13th. On the evening of 13th the Battalion was relieved by 13th Cameron Highlanders & moved back into Divisional Reserve at HUDDLESTON CAMP. Total casualties for period in front line 17 O.R. wounded, of whom 2 subsequently died.	
HUDDLESTON CAMP	13/3/18 to 17/3/18		A very quiet period spent in Reserve, with most excellent weather. A little work was done on Lewis and Rifle Range but otherwise resting. Battalion moved up into Support area on the evening of 17th, but with 2 Coys in full bcoa around LANGEMARCK, and 1 Company in huts near GOURNIER FARM and 1 Company and Bn HQs in KEMPTON PARK.	
KEMPTON PARK	17/3/18 to 21/3/18		Period in Support area was fairly quiet - quieter than the Reserve area which we had just left, where the Cameron had one hut blown up and several more damaged. Owing to shelling of the back area Support Companies employed in working on the forward area nightly.	

Army Form C. 2118.

WAR DIARY
or
INTELLIGENCE SUMMARY.
(Erase heading not required.)

Instructions regarding War Diaries and Intelligence Summaries are contained in F. S. Regs., Part II. and the Staff Manual respectively. Title pages will be prepared in manuscript.

Place	Date	Hour	Summary of Events and Information	Remarks and references to Appendices
KEMPTON PARK	21-3-18		Battalion moved up in the evening and relieved 1st & 2nd The Black Watch	
SOUVENIR HOUSE	22-3-18		Dispositions R F D Coy, L F C Coy, Support B Coy, Reserve A Coy	ft
	24-3-18		Sector which had become somewhat unhealthy during our period in Support and Reserve, quietened down again almost immediately. Active patrolling of our front was carried out with a view of raiding enemy posts. Inter Company Relief was carried out on night of 23/24th as before A & B Coys	
			interchanging with C & D Coys respectively	ft
SOUVENIR HOUSE	25-3-18		The enemy post at GRAVEL FARM @ V.8.A.00 was finally decided on as the objective of our raid, and the raid was carried out in the early morning of March 25th in accordance with attached orders ×	× A.
			The raid was successfully carried out; 1 wounded prisoner 1 Company 103 R.I.R being captured and 3 other enemy killed. Our casualties were 2 or slightly wounded. (Fuller report attached *)	*B.
			In the evening the Battalion was relieved by 1st Cameron Highlanders and moved back to very comfortable billets in the canal Bank astride BARDS CAUSEWAY. (B. 19. A. 17.)	ft

Army Form C. 2118.

WAR DIARY
or
INTELLIGENCE SUMMARY.
(Erase heading not required.)

Instructions regarding War Diaries and Intelligence Summaries are contained in F. S. Regs., Part II. and the Staff Manual respectively. Title pages will be prepared in manuscript.

Place	Date	Hour	Summary of Events and Information	Remarks and references to Appendices
CANAL BANK	26/3/18 to 28/3/18		A very peaceful and comfortable period spent in Reserve resting and bathing, except on the last day when 2 Companies had to be found for work on the Army line. A draft of 30 O.R. joined the Battalion on 28th. In the evening of the 29th the Battalion moved up into the Support area. Dispositions as follows :- 2 Companies in LANGEMARCK area two & platoons disposed as Support System to forward zone of A Coy (HQ PG + Whistles) in WHITEMILL and LOUIS FARM, and of B Coy (HQ LANGEMARCK STATION) in EAGLE TRENCH + BEAR LOCALITY. (the 2 Companies (C + D) and Bn HQs in CAINE TRENCH around C.9 Central. Two Companies working each night on wire of forward area. 2nd Lieut G.G. Claridge joined the Battalion 29th. from 7th Loyal Lancs R.	V
CAINE TRENCH	30/3/18 to 31/3/18		Fighting strength of Battalion on 31st March was :- 47 Officers. 1009. O.R.s.	

1-4-18

A.C. Phillips Lieut. Col.
Commdg. 1st Bn. Loyal N. Lancashire Regt.

SECRET.

1st LOYAL NORTH LANCS. REGIMENT ORDER No. 89.

1. **OPERATION.**
   'B' Coy. with Artillery Support will carry out a reconnaissance of enemy posts around GRAVEL FARM on night 24th/25th March.

2. **OBJECTIVES.**
   (i) To kill enemy.
   (ii) To obtain identifications by Prisoners or papers etc. off the dead.

3. **STRENGTH.**
   Patrol will consist of 2nd Lt. C DIBLEY, Sgt. CLANCY, M.M. 1 runner and 3 Sections each of 1 L.O.C. and 6 men.

4. **DRESS.**
   Rifle and bayonet, 10 rounds magazine and 25 rounds S.A.A. in pocket.
   Wire cutters will be carried by all personnel of raid H.Qs. and 3 by each Section. TOTAL:- 12.
   All papers and identification marks of all kind will be removed from the patrol before starting including identity discs.
   Special identity discs will be issued this evening.

5. **COVERING PARTY.**
   A flanking party of 3 Sections under 2nd Lt. WHITEHEAD will be disposed as under:-
   (i) 2nd Lt. WHITEHEAD with 2 Sections will accompany the raiding party up to WATERVLIETBEEK & take up a position astride BEEK, 1 Section riflemen on North bank, and 1 Section L.G. on S. bank, both facing EAST.
   (ii) Third Section (L.G.) will take up a position on road about V.8.c.4.4. also facing EAST.

6. **PROGRAMME.**
   (i) ZERO - 15. Patrol and covering party (i) will assemble about 50 yds. South of WATERVLIETBEEK about V.8.c.?.7. Covering party (ii) will be in position as detailed.
   (ii) ZERO. Artillery and M.Gs. open as per programmes 'A' and 'B' attached.
   (iii) ZERO + 5. Artillery lifts, patrol & covering party (i) cross, and patrol will advance into GRAVEL Fm.
   (iv) ZERO + 20. Patrol will withdraw, recall signal to be given by 2nd Lt. DIBLEY by 3 blasts on whistle.
   (v) ZERO + 25. Patrol will be withdrawn across BEEK and return to BOWE R.
   2nd Lt. WHITEHEAD will check numbers of patrol as they return and as soon as all have passed through will withdraw, followed by covering party (ii).

7. **PRISONERS.**
   All Prisoners taken by patrol will be sent back immediately to BOWER, where they will be taken over by 'B' Coy. and sent down to Hd. Qrs.
   'C' Coy. will hold escort in readiness to take them on if required.

8. **IDENTIFICATIONS.**
   Two men of each section of patrol will be told off to search all dead for papers, identity discs and shoulder straps. These will be collected and sent to Hd. Qrs. as early as possible after return.

(2)

9. MEDICAL.
4 S.Bs. of 'B' Coy. will move with 2nd Lt. WHITEHEAD'S covering party.
4 S.Bs. of 'D' Coy will be at BOWER House.
4 S.Bs. of 'C' Coy. will be at IMBROS House.

Each stretcher bearer will carry up 1 stretcher to above points.

10. COMMUNICATION.
By runner from patrol H.Q. to Forward Coy. H.Q. ('B' Coy.) at BOWER House.
Thence (i) By direct line to Bn. H.Q.
(ii) By runner to MILLERS and thence by Coy. line.

11. 2nd Lt. WHITEHEAD will be provided with electric lamp with red disc which will be flashed every few seconds from ZERO + 20 onwards until patrol have returned, to guide patrol back to crossing point.

12. Synchronised time will be sent round to all immediately concerned about 9-0 p.m.

13. ZERO hour will be 4-30 a.m. 25th March.

14. ACKNOWLEDGE.

J Lindsell
Captain & Adjt.
1st Loyal North Lancs. Regiment.

24th March 1918.

Copies to:-

'A' Coy.
'B' Coy.
'C' Coy.
'D' Coy.
Officer i/c Patrol.
C.O.
Signals.
1st Inf. Bde.
Office (2).

APPENDIX 'A'.

UNIT.	1st PHASE. ZERO to ZERO plus 5.			2nd PHASE. ZERO plus 5 to ZERO plus 35.				3rd PHASE. ZERO plus 35 to ZERO plus 55.		
	No. of guns.	Targets.	Rds. p.g.p.m.	No. of guns.	Targets.	Rds. p.g. p.m.	No. of guns.	Targets.	No. of guns.	Rds. p.g. p.m.
124	6	Line of posts 7.S.a.05.00. to V.8.c.25.90. (Shrapnel with 1 rd.in 4 smoke).	4	6	Barrage Line V.8.a.2.3. to 7.S. a.5.7. (50% A. 50% A.X.)	1	6	Machine guns Group F.	1	
125	3	CREEPING BARRAGE starting on line V.7.d.95.05. to V.8.c.15.65.05.86 advancing 25 yds per min. to line of posts V.8.a.05.00. to V.8.c.20.65. (shrapnel).	4	6	VAN DYCK FM.* (Counter prepara-tion area marked green) 50% A. 50% AX	1	6	Remain on VAN DYCK Fm.	1	
A/36.	6	BARRAGE ROAD V.8.c.0.0. to V.8.c.24.20. All M.G.	4	6	Barrage on line 100 yds. N. of & parallel to road at V.8.c.0.0. to V.8.c.24.20.	12	6	Machine Guns Group D.	1	
35 HOWS.	1	ZERO to ZERO plus 5. Line of posts V.8.a.05.00. to V.8.c.20.85.(Smoke)	2	3	ZERO to ZERO plus 30. RUBENS Fm. V.8.c.80.75.- BX. 7.S.c.9.3. V.7.b.2.7. 7.S.a.55.45. } B.X.A.	1	4	Remain as in phase 2.	1	
	1	ZERO plus 5 to ZERO plus 30. VAN DYCK FM.(B.A.A.) Zero is Zero + 4.			Zero + 4 to Zero + 30 V.7.b.7.5.					

* At ZERO plus 5, 135 Battery will commence lifting by 100 yards on to VAN DYCK FM. where it will remain searching and sweeping.

APPENDIX 'B'.

	GUNS.	TARGETS.
I.	2 guns at G.18.b.70.10.	V.2.c.10.05. - V.2.c.35.10. and V.2.c.35.10. - V.8.a.95.80.
II.	2 guns at U.24.b.80.75.	V.8.a.95.80. to V.8.b.15.40. and V.8.b.15.40. to V.8.d.20.80.

Rate of fire will be:-

ZERO to ZERO plus 10.	100 rds. p.g.p.m.
ZERO plus 10 to plus 20.	bursts of 50 rds. p.g.p.m.
ZERO plus 20 to plus 40.	Bursts of 40 rounds every 5 minutes.

REPORT ON RAID CARRIED OUT BY "B" COMPANY, 1st BATTALION
LOYAL NORTH LANCASHIRE REGIMENT IN THE EARLY MORNING OF
MARCH 25th, 1918.

The raiding party consisting of 2/Lieut. Dibley, Sergt. Clancy, M.M., and 22 Other Ranks reached the assembling point at the WATERVLIETBEEK at V.8.c.2.8. without anything unusal happening at 4-35a.m.

Party crossed the stream at this point by Trench Boards placed across the stream for this purpose.

The party then advanced to within 40 yards of GRAVEL FARM when one row of wire was encountered about 3 feet high, and in a fair condition.

A small party headed by Corp. LANCASTER struck a gap and rushed forward.

Corp. Lancaster was grappled with by 2 of the enemy, but these were both killed by Sergt. Clancy, M.M., who was following close behind. Two more of the enemy then approached, of whom one was killed and the other captured. Four more of the enemy fled in a Northeasterly direction.

The enemy appeared to be taken completely by surprise, and appeared to have no means of resisting an attack from this flank.

The enemy position consisted of a small Pill Box with a breastwork Trench running to a small Dugout or cellar in the ruins of the farm.

No enemy S.O.S. was sent up, nor was there any retaliation to our barrage.

The prisoner captured belonged to the 1st Company, 103rd R.I.R., 58th Division.

The patrol, closely followed by the covering party, returned to our lines at 4-55a.m.

Our casualties were - two other ranks slightly wounded.

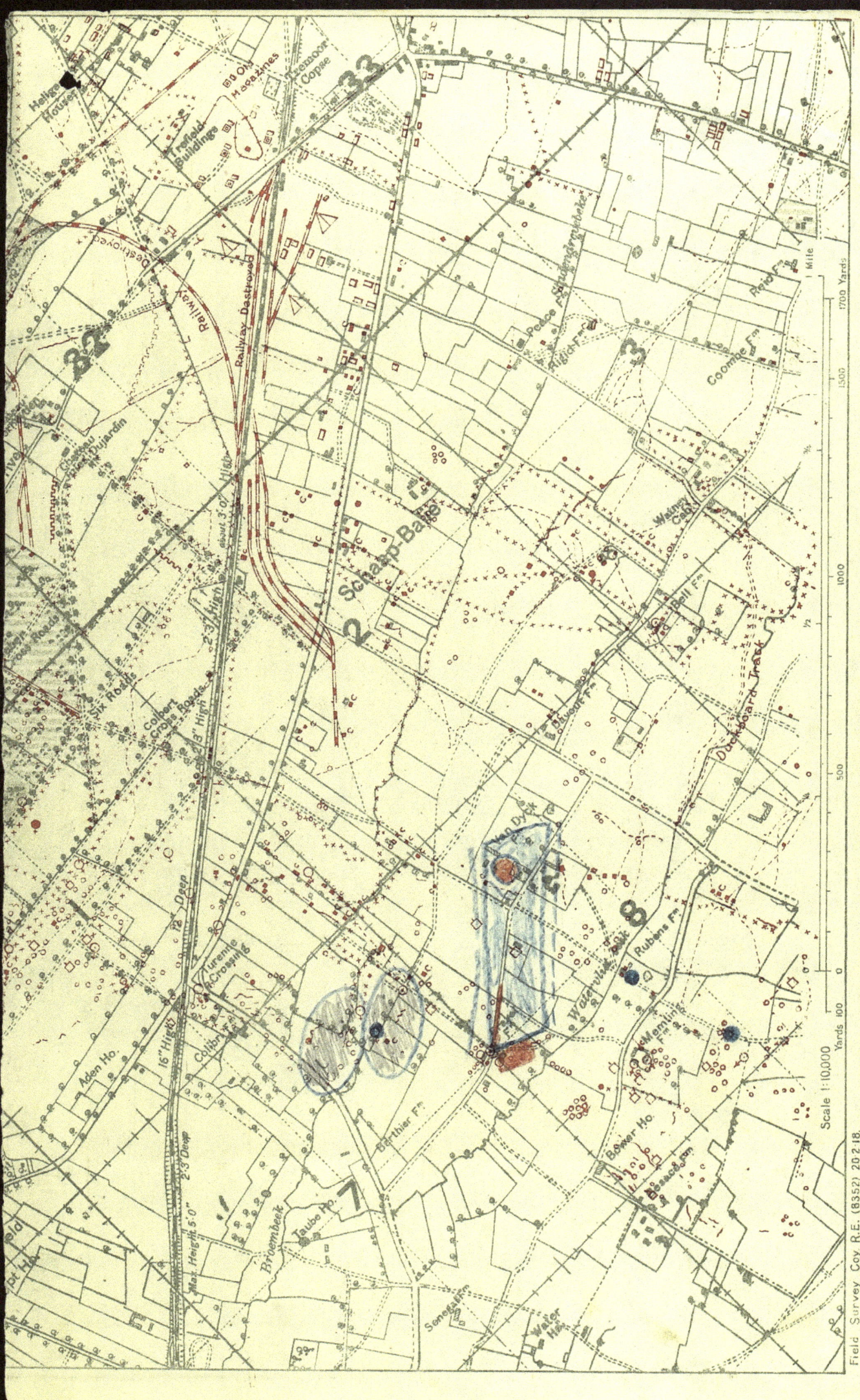

1st Brigade.
1st Division.

1st BATTALION

LOYAL NORTH LANCASHIRE REGIMENT

APRIL 1918.

WAR DIARY or INTELLIGENCE SUMMARY

Army Form C. 2118.

1st Battalion The Royal North Lancashire Regt.

April 1918

Place	Date	Hour	Summary of Events and Information	Remarks and references to Appendices
CPRE TRENCH	1/IV/18 to 2/IV/18		Nothing of importance occurred. Enemy generally quiet on the front. Bn relieved the 1st The Black Watch on the night of the 2nd/3rd, relief being completed at 3.10 A.M. Bn frontage extended from the YPRES-STADEN Railway on the North to BESACE on the South. Dispositions of Coys - D left, C right, A support, B Reserve. Relief was carried out without anything unusual occurring. 2 casualties (slight) were caused by M.G. fire.	HDS
In the Line SOUVENIR FARM U.18.c.3.6.	3/IV/18 to 6/IV/18		Little enemy activity on the front. Certain amount of T.M. & M.G. Fire directed against the left coy front without causing much damage. Hostile Artillery was slight & scattered with exception of EAGLE Trench which was fairly consistently shelled. No guns or trench cellos were used. An inter-company relief was carried out on the night of the 4/5th without incident. On the early morning of the 6th an offensive patrol consisting of 2/Lt French Stewart & 20 O.R's left our line at BESACE FARM with a view to obtain an identification. They proceeded in an Easterly direction for a distance of 150 yards. They were unable to locate any of the enemy and returned to our line.	HR
-do-	7/IV/18		Two fighting patrols were sent out in an endeavor to obtain identification HR	

WAR DIARY 1st Bn. The Loyal North Lancashire Regt.
or
INTELLIGENCE SUMMARY.

Army Form C. 2118.

April 1918

Place	Date	Hour	Summary of Events and Information	Remarks and references to Appendices
	7/4/18		Patrols were not successful. Copy of orders issued prior to Bn. are attached. Bn. was relieved on the night of the 7th. 3 Coys by the 18th King's Liverpool Regt. remaining Coy by the 17th King's Liverpool Regt. Relief completed at 11.45 pm. Bn. arrived in billets at WHITEMILL CAMP ELVERDINGHE at 3.15 AM	A88
	8/4/18		Bn. moved by march route thence to "LAPUGNOY", leaving ELVERDINGHE at 5.5 pm + arrived in billets at "LAPUGNOY" about 3AM on the 9th	A88
9/4/18	LAPUGNOY		Day devoted to rest. Bn. was at 2 hours notice from 10.30 AM to 1.30 pm	
	10/4/18		Day spent in cleaning up when necessary & general reorganisation of Coys. C.O. & Coy cmdrs reconnoitred the reserve defences E. of Bethune. Details to be left out of the line (about 260 all ranks) proceeded to billets in Bn. Bure.	A88
	11/4/18	HOUCHIN	Bn. moved by Buses to Houchin arriving about 5pm.	A88
	12/4/18 to 15/4/18	BEUVRY	Moved by march route to BEUVRY leaving camp about 11.30 pm arriving in billets in BEUVRY about 3 pm. Owing to hostile shelling of the village, which at times was very severe, all ranks were confined to billets so far as possible	A88

WAR DIARY
or
INTELLIGENCE SUMMARY

(Erase heading not required.)

Army Form C. 2118.

Place	Date	Hour	Summary of Events and Information	Remarks and references to Appendices
			accomodated in the cellars. During the 3 days occupation of BEUVRY 10 casualties were sustained - chiefly of a light nature. Positions were reconnoitred with a view to forming a defence in case of hostile attack from either the N. or E.	
LE PREOL	15/IV/18		Bn relieved the 1st Gloster in the defences of LE PREOL. Relief completed about 10.30 pm.	hR.
On the line	16/IV/18 17/IV/18		The Bn moved forward into the sector LA BASSEE CANAL northwards to A.14.a.9.5.9.5. Taking over from the 2/5 Lancashire Fusiliers. Disposition of Coy's from right to left. C - B - A - D Coy in support - Bn Hq at A.14.a.9.0.8.0. The day was dull relief was carried out in daylight - only one casualty being sustained. Relief completed at 3.55 pm. Day generally quiet.	hR.
	18/IV/18		At 4.15 AM the enemy commenced to bombard the whole of the Dn Front. The barrage became intense & at 8.10 the enemy attacked from the N. filtering into our trenches under cover of the high ground at GIVENCHY. He succeeded in reaching & reoccupying the main line of resistance before counter measures could be taken. Vigorous counter attacks by C & D Coys	hR.

Army Form C. 2118.

WAR DIARY
or
INTELLIGENCE SUMMARY.
(Erase heading not required.)

Instructions regarding War Diaries and Intelligence Summaries are contained in F. S. Regs., Part II. and the Staff Manual respectively. Title pages will be prepared in manuscript.

Place	Date	Hour	Summary of Events and Information	Remarks and references to Appendices
In the line			eventually succeeded in ejecting the enemy from own main line by 11 AM. he was only holding a few isolated posts in our outpost line.	
	19/11/18		Beyond a certain amount of sniping the day was fairly quiet	A/S
	20/11/18		In the early morning the 1st Bn Northamptons carried out an attack to regain the old positions + portions of the French line in front of CHENERY.	A/S
	21/11/18 to 23/11/18		Remainder of period was fairly quiet though was concentrated an unpressing the defensive system. The Bn was relieved on the night of the 23/24th by the 1/4 Kings Own R. Lancaster Regt. + moved back by bus from ANNEQUIN to HOUCHIN. Relief completed without incident at 1.30 am. Casualties during period were Lieut King, Petitt killed, Capts Bere MC, Capt Jeffreys, 2Lieut Bell, 2Lieut Mallett, Lieut Allen wounded, Capt Smith MC, L. Cladding, 2Lieuts Smith, Claridge + Whitehead missing. 46 ORs killed 105 wounded 189 ORs missing 6 ORs	A/S

Army Form C. 2118.

WAR DIARY
or
INTELLIGENCE SUMMARY.
(Erase heading not required.)

Instructions regarding War Diaries and Intelligence Summaries are contained in F. S. Regs., Part II. and the Staff Manual respectively. Title pages will be prepared in manuscript.

Place	Date	Hour	Summary of Events and Information	Remarks and references to Appendices
HOUCHIN	24/1/18		The Bn moved into billets in NOEUX les MINES arriving in about	
		3.30 PM		
NOEUX les MINES	25/1/18		Period employed in reorganising the Bn, training of Lewis Gunners et & general training. Draft of 21 ORs joined the Bn on	
	to		the 27th. Lt Col. PHILIPS DSO MC. went to rest camp at WIMEREUX on	
	30/1/18		the 29th + Major Bullock took over command of the Bn.	
			Officers joined during the month :- Capt LEAKE M.C. Lt SANDIE M.C.	
			2 Lieuts HOWARD, HARDY, MOYKOPF, PARDOE, HORROCKS, WHITEHEAD, on the	
			22nd. 2/Lieut PAGE WOOD on the 29th.	

G.A. Bullock
Major.
cmdg. 1/L.N. Lancs Regt.

30/1/18

SECRET

1st Bn L N Lancs Rt

Operations Orders - Night of 6/7th April

General Idea

1. "A" & "D" Coys will each send fighting patrols on nights of 6/7th

"A" Coys party consisting of Lt Ward 3 Sections
& small covering party
"D"   "   "   Lt McLean & 4 Sutwins

Sgt Roskell & 3 Scouts will comprise the covering party for "A" Coy

Object of patrols - to obtain identification of the enemy opposite the front and to kill any of the enemy seen they are unable to capture

II Special Idea

(a) "A" Coys patrol
Patrol will leave our lines about V 8 C 12 at 2 am & proceed along hedge to the Watervliet Beek at V 8 C 28

The Beek will be crossed by duckboards. The patrol will then proceed NNW and endeavour to capture the Garrison of Gravel Farm situated about V 8 C 05·95 which consists of 8 men and a light MG.

Signal for withdrawal will be given by Lt Ward.

Covering party will be responsible for carrying the duckboards forward and laying them across the Beek and bringing them in when patrol has returned.

Artillery Programme

From 2.15 am to 2.35 am one Howitzer will fire 1 round per min using 106 fuse. The object of this is to cover the noise of the patrol placing the duckboards crossing the beek and approaching

"D" Coys patrol.

Patrol will leave our lines from point V 17 b 2.2 at 2.35 am & proceed N along the TURENNE crossing road to where the Broembeek crosses the road

At 2.50 am the patrol will proceed along the Broembeek and endeavour to obtain identification

One section will remain at the point where the Broembeek crosses the Road & act as a Covering party.

Artillery Programme

At 2.45 am 2 batteries of 18 pdrs will barrage from V7 b 55 50 to 55 65 and V7 b 55 50 to 90.55 using mostly shrapnel. Rate of fire 3 rounds per gun per minute.

At 2.50 am barrage will creep at 50' per minute to line V7 b 55 65 – V7 b 90 80 – V7 b 70 60.

They will cease fire at 3.5 am

General Instructions

(a) <u>Marks of Identification</u>

All marks of identification & papers will be removed before the patrols quit our lines.

Special raid identity discs will be issued this evening

(b) **Equipment**

Each man will carry Rifle & Bayonet & 20 rounds SAA (10 rounds in magazine and 10 in pocket) & two pairs of wire cutters per Section. No other equipment will be taken.

C. **Evacuation of Casualties**

"A" Coys patrol – SBs of "A" Coy will accompany the patrol & remain with the covering party. "C" Coys SBs will be stationed at Bowers House & Reserve Bearers at Compromise thus forming 3 relay posts.

"D" Coy patrol. 2 SBs will accompany the patrol and remain with the covering party. They will carry to Tambe and then hand over to "B" Coys SB

(d) **Company HQ**

"A" Coy Hd will move to Bowers House for purposes of the enterprise. OC "A" Coy will be responsible for calling the roll on the return of the patrol and reporting any casualties immediately and for sending down the prisoners captured, under escort, to Bn HQ. He will also send down by wire to Bn HQ the Company, Regt and Division of the Prisoners Captured

(e) Each patrol will tell off men specially for the purpose of removing shoulder straps and other marks of identification from any of the enemy who may be killed

(f) Acknowledge.

N. Douglas Stthayer
Lieut
6/4/18   Adjt 1st Lafans Rt.

Copies to
O.C. "A" Coy   Lt Ward.
" "B" "   Lt McLean.
" "C" "   Office
" "D" "   War Diary

Operation Orders

1. The Battalion will attack in conjunction with the 2 Bde on the left and the 18th Bde on the right at an hour on "Z" day to be notified later. The Bn will attack on the right with the Camerons on the left and the Black Watch in Reserve.

2. Objectives and Bn boundaries have already been communicated to Coy Commrs. 1st and 2nd Objectives will be gained under cover of a creeping barrage. The 3rd objective will be gained by exploitation after 2nd objective has been gained.

3. On Y/Z night the RE will tape out a forming up line in accordance with the map co-ordinates submitted by this front Corps. The Bn will form up on a two Coy front - "C" on the left "D" on the right - on the taped line. A & B Coy will be disposed in depth in rear. A Coy in area R 29 d and R 36 a, B Coy in area now occupied by A Coy

4/ One Section TM Battery will move forward with A Coy. In event of their assistance being required O.C. C & D Coys will communicate direct with OC A Coy.

One Section A Coy MG Bn will move under orders of B HQ.

5/ Barrage Programme:-
(a) 18 Pdr Barrage will come down 200x in front of forming up line at Zero hour 4.5 How Barrage will come down 200x beyond 18 Pdr Barrage
(b) Artillery lifts will be 100x
(c) First lift will be at Zero + 3 mins at which hour the Infantry will advance to the crossnet.
Second lift will be at Zero plus 5. From 3rd to 11th lift all lifts will be at 4 mins interval
(d) There will be a halt on the 1st objective from Zero plus 1 hour 12 mins to Zero plus 3 hours 10 mins

At Zero plus 3 hours 10 mins the advance will be continued to the 2nd objective. On reaching the protective barrage 2nd objective Artillery will continue firing 15 minutes after which it will stop until S.O.S is required.

(c) For 2 hours after protective barrage 2nd objective stops no field artillery will be available to support further advance

6. Light Signals:
S.O.S. Signal will be a rifle grenade bursting into 3 red lights (Red, Red, Red) Success signal (signifying that 2nd objective has been gained) will be rifle grenade bursting into 3 white lights (White, White, White) which will be fired from B.H.Q.

7. Contact Aeroplanes:-
(a) A Contact aeroplane will fly along the front and call for flares and showing of discs by sounding a Klaxon Horn half

an hour after troops are due on 1st and 2nd Objectives respectively viz at Zero plus 102 mins and Zero plus 204 mins (metal discs are being issued

(b) The following method of giving warning of a counter attack will be employed by Aeroplanes. Aeroplane will fly in the direction of the enemy dropping a white parachute flare as near the counter attacking troops as possible

7. Lines of advance :-
C Coy will advance to the 1st objective with the left flank on a true bearing of 50° (taken from point R 30 a 5.5. to point M 20 b 25 80.
From the 1st to the 2nd objectives the left flank will move on a true bearing of 61° (taken from point M 20 b 25 80 to M 16 a 70 75.

D Coy will advance to the 1st objective with the right flank on a true bearing of 54° (taken from point M 26 C 30 75 to M 21 C 80 55 from the 1st to the 2nd objectives the right flank will move on a true bearing of 57° (taken from point M 21 c 80 55 to M 16 d 10 00) From the Jumping off position to the 1st Objective the inter Coy boundary will be on a true bearing of 52° (taken from point M 25 b 6 of to point M 21 a 15 30) From 1st to 2nd objectives inter Coy boundary will be on a true bearing of 61° (taken from point M 21 a 15 30 to M 16 c 75 70) Left and Right front Coys will arrange for Officer Compass parties to move on their left and right flanks respectively on the bearings given above. These bearings must be carefully checked.

On gaining the 2nd objective front Coys will each send forward 1 platoon to establish themselves on the 3rd objective

During the advance the right Coy will establish touch with the right flank Bn

at the following points:-
(a) FRESNOY Trench at   M 21 c 8 5
(b) Trench at   M 22 a 0 4
(c) DAVID Trench at   M 22 a 8 9
(d) SAMPSON Trench at   M 16 d 0 0

Bn Hqrs will move as follows:-
Zero - 15 mins will be established in Sunken Road R. 34. b. 5. 9. At Zero will move forward to vicinity of ESSLING ALLEY in R 30 a. Further moves will be made in accordance with situation

9. The 3rd Objective is amended East of M 10 b 2. 4 to run M 10 b 2.4. to M 11 c 0. 0. to M 17. c. 0. 8. where it gains 2nd objective on 6th Div front

10. The firing of White very lights on the 1st. and 2nd objectives being gained: as decided at Coy Commrs conference will NOT be carried out

11. Synchronisation of watches will be carried out at BHQ at 5 pm and 10 pm today. One Officer per Coy., M.G.C. & T M B Officers will attend

12. C & D Coy Commrs will render all the assistance they can to the RE in taping out the forming up line
Actual forming up line will be given later
Administrative orders will be issued separately
Zero will be notified later

W. Douglas Stephenson
Capt
17/9/18

C O P Y.

Headquarters,
1st Infantry Brigade.

1   REPORT ON FIGHTING PATROLS CARRIED OUT ON THE
                        NIGHT 6/7th APRIL.

1. PATROL AGAINST GRAVEL POST.

Patrol consisting of Lt. WARD and 20 O. Rs. left our lines from V.8.c.1.2. and proceeded along the hedge to the WATERVLIET BEEK. Very lights were continually fired in this direction during this time. Duckboards were placed across the BEEK, and the party crossed without casualties. They then proceeded in three lines at about 20 yards interval in a N.N.W. direction towards the post. When the parties got within 15 yards of the enemy wire, the barrage on the left opened. The enemy had a party working on the wire when the barrage commenced, and they immediately retired behind the wire and stood to. Very lights were put up by the enemy, and they immediately opened fire on our party with 2 Machine Guns, rifle fire and bombs. Twenty of the enemy were counted behind the wire.

The patrol moved in to within 10 yards working round to the right, hoping to locate a gap in the wire. This effort met with no success, and a number of casualties were sustained.

A lively exchange of rifle fire took place - a few bombs were thrown by us and Lieut. WARD fired several shots from his revolver. As there was no possible chance of rushing the wire (which consisted of 3 rows of concertina wire filled in with balls of barbed wire) the party then withdrew; arriving in our lines about 4.25a.m.

During the whole time the patrol was out, the enemy fired very lights towards the gap in our wire at V.8.c.1.2. (the point from which the patrol left our lines) as far as can be ascertained at the present time, our casualties are - Lt. WARD (seriously wounded) and 5 O. Rs. wounded.

A further report on this patrol will be forwarded, if any fresh details are revealed.

BROEMBEEK PATROL.

Patrol consisted of 2/Lt. McLean and 20 O. Rs.
They left our lines from V.17.b.2.2. at 2.35a.m. and proceeded N. along the TURENNE crossing road to point where the BROEMBEEK crossed the road.

They remained here until 2.50a.m.
At 2.45a.m. the artillery and M. G. barrage opened.
At 2.50a.m. the patrol moved forward along the BROEMBEEK with the object of obtaining an identification. No enemy were encountered; it was not possible to cross the BEEK owing to the swampy state of the ground, and patrol according withdrew in accordance with orders issued.

This patrol sustained no casualties.
The artillery and M. G. barrage was entirely satisfactory.

                                    (Signed) N. Douglas Stephenson, Lieut.,
7/4/18.   for Lt. Col. Commanding, 1st Loyal N. Lancs. Regiment.

SECRET

WAR DIARY
or
INTELLIGENCE SUMMARY

Army Form C. 2118.

1st Northamptons

Vol 45

Place	Date	Hour	Summary of Events and Information	Remarks and references to Appendices
NOEUX Les MINES.	MAY 1st		Company Specialist training continued	A08
	2nd		Bn relieved the 1st Bn. The Northamptonshire Regt in the CAMBRIN SECTOR on night 2nd Bn. Owing to lack of numbers A & B Coys were amalgamated in one coy. Disposition in the line :- A Coys - Left front Coy. B Coy - right front Coy. C Coy - Right Support Coy. one Coy of 2nd/1 R.R. Corps attached - left support coy. 2 platoons of the Black Watch manning Leven KEEP + Manin Range post. Relief was completed without incident at 11.30pm	
	3rd to		Sector very quiet + peaceful - the enemy severely replied to the harassing fire of our artillery machine guns. Strong patrols were sent out nightly but were unable to engage the enemy, who apparently retired when our patrol were sighted. 30 reinforcements joined the Bn in the line on the 6th + 30 on the 8th enabling	A08
	9th to		A + B to reform as two companies before the coy attacked the 10th, 11th, + 12th	
	10th to		Enemy still very inactive. On the nights of the 10th, 11th, + 12th preparations were made to discharge gas at the enemy from our position. However owing to unfavourable winds the	A08
	12th			

WAR DIARY
or
INTELLIGENCE SUMMARY.
(Erase heading not required.)

Army Form C. 2118.

Place	Date	Hour	Summary of Events and Information	Remarks and references to Appendices
	13th to 21st Sept.		operation did not take place, until the night of the 13th. S97 Projectors were successfully fired into the enemy's rear position in front of AUCHY at 10.30pm on the 13th. Five minutes elapsed before the enemy made any reply. The reply was feeble started only to suruile owing to the favourable weather, aerial activity on both sides increased considerably. Strong patrols were continually sent out but had no success.	MDS
	22nd		The Bn was relieved by the 1st Bn GLOUCESTER Regt & moved back into billets in NOEUX les MINES. Relief was carried out in daylight & completed without incident at 7.30pm	MDS
NOEUX les MINES	23rd.		Day devoted to bathing & general cleaning up	
	24th to 27th		During training special attention was devoted to the tactical training of the Platoon. Musketry & Lewis Guns training were also given special attention afterwards	MDS

Army Form C. 2118.

WAR DIARY
or
INTELLIGENCE SUMMARY.
(Erase heading not required.)

Instructions regarding War Diaries and Intelligence Summaries are contained in F. S. Regs., Part II. and the Staff Manual respectively. Title pages will be prepared in manuscript.

Place	Date	Hour	Summary of Events and Information	Remarks and references to Appendices
In the line	MAY 28th		Bn relieved the 2nd Royal Sussex Regt on left Bn HOHENZOLLERN Sector Relief was carried out in daylight & completed at 7.40 p.m. Disposition of Companies – Left front B Coy Right front D Coy Support A Coy Reserve C Coy	
	29th & 31st		On the whole the sector was fairly quiet. Beyond occasional "Areas Shoots" the enemy made little reply to our harassing fires. Patrols were sent out but were unable to engage the enemy.	h88 h88
			Reinforcements during the month – Officers – 2/Lieut J.R. McHUGH – joined 9/5/18. 2/Lt A. GILLINGHAM – joined 13/5/18. 2/Lt F. JAMES – joined 18-5-18. Capt G.W AINSWORTH – joined 20-5-18. 2/Lieut J.C WRIGHT joined 24-5-18. Lt D F POLLARD – rejoined 27-5-18 recalled from home & taught duty at home Other Ranks – 51 ORs joined 3/5/18 80 ORs 6/5/18 22 ORs 9/5/18 12 ORs 20/5/18	
			Casualties during the month 1 Offr & 10 ORs wounded 1 OR killed Extracts from Bn Orders (attached) shew decoration awarded for gallantry at GIVENCHY 13/4/18.	

D.C. Phillips
Lieut. Col.
Commdg. 1st Bn. Loyal N. Lancashire Regt.

EXTRACTS FROM BATTALION ORDERS 1ST BATTALION LOYAL NORTH LANCASHIRE REGIMENT.

No 7. of 22/5/18. HONOURS AND REWARDS

The Commanding Officer has great pleasure in announcing that under authority delegated by His Majesty the King the Field Marshal Commanding-in-Chief has awarded the following decorations:-

THE DISTINGUISHED SERVICE ORDER

Captain   A.R.Bare, M.C.,
Captain   A.B.Bratton M.C.,

THE MILITARY CROSS

2/Lieut   J.S.Fiddes
2/Lieut   J.H.F.Bell.
Lieut (a/Capt) A.H.Jefferys (Middlesex Regt attached)

THE DISTINGUISHED CONDUCT MEDAL.

18551 Sergt (a/ C.S.M.) R.Thomas
16746 Sergt   T.Davies
22055 L/Sergt   R.Davies   (now Sergeant)
22193 L/Corpl.   O.Jones M.M., (Now L/Sergt)

THE MILITARY MEDAL (BAR TO)

35556 Pte G.Arandle M.M.   11525 Pte S.Bades M.M.
22045 " W.Dooner M.M.   17450 " J.Brewer M.M.

THE MILITARY MEDAL.

18825 Cpl E.Bevan   22568 Pte A.Hadfield
26050 Pte J.Greenaway   25825 " J.F.Harney
8846 L/C W.Sayers   2527   " J.Winsper
16547 Sgt P.Higson   25558 L/C A.H.Livesey
17558 Pte A.Howarth   26599 Pte W.Pattison
201480 " W.Hindle   26645 " T.Rodgers
28688 " G.Haskins   35612 " J.Benn
22575 " J.Kuhn   24158 L/C J.Watson (now Corpl)

5 of 27/5/18. HONOURS AND AWARDS.

The Commanding Officer has great pleasure in announcing that under authority delegated by His Majesty the King the Field Marshal Commanding-in-Chief has awarded the MILITARY CROSS to
          2nd Lieut E.T.MALLETT 1st L.N.Lancashire Regiment.

SECRET

Army Form C. 2118.

6 L N Lane Bn
June 1918

SVL 46

WAR DIARY
or
INTELLIGENCE SUMMARY.
(Erase heading not required.)

Instructions regarding War Diaries and Intelligence Summaries are contained in F. S. Regs., Part II. and the Staff Manual respectively. Title pages will be prepared in manuscript.

Place	Date	Hour	Summary of Events and Information	Remarks and references to Appendices
HOHENZOLLERN Sub	1/6/18		Quiet day. Bn was relieved by the Cameron Highlanders & moved back into support in Annequin. Relief completed without casualties at 11.40pm	
ANNEQUIN	2/6/18 to 4/6/18		Very quiet time. An average of 100 men were found daily for working parties. A certain amount of musketry & specialist training was carried out. The Bn less 5 platoons relieved 1/5 The Black Watch less 5 platoons in the right Bn sector. Resp 1st platoons of D Coy were left behind in Annequin under Lt.Col. Phillips D.S.O. M.C. for the purpose of practising a Raid. Major Buttock took the Bn into the line.	hqs hqs hqs
HOHENZOLLERN Sub	5/6/18			
	6/6/18		Enemy artillery & T.Ms were fairly active against our forward system. No casualties were sustained. Aeroplane activity normal.	
	7/6/18		Fairly heavy T.M fire was carried by both sides. A reconnoitring patrol consisting of Capt Leake M.C Lt French +3 ORs which left our line at 12.30AM was driven back by an enemy pat. Two men were wounded + an enemy. Every effort was made to recover the latter without success	hqs
	8/6/18 9/6/18		Enemy artillery, T.M & aeroplane activity below normal. Little reply was made to our harassing fire	hqs

Army Form C. 2118.

WAR DIARY
or
INTELLIGENCE SUMMARY.
(Erase heading not required.)

June 1918

Instructions regarding War Diaries and Intelligence Summaries are contained in F. S. Regs., Part II. and the Staff Manual respectively. Title pages will be prepared in manuscript.

Place	Date	Hour	Summary of Events and Information	Remarks and references to Appendices
HOHENZOLLERN Sector	10/6/18		Quiet day. Bray's Raid cancelled & company moved into the line, relieving the Company of the Black Watch attacked. Lt. Col. Phillips took over command of the line & Major Bottcock was sent down to hospital.	
	11/6/18		Enemy activity normal. Preparations were made to carry out a raid with 3 companies A,B, & D being selected.	H.S.
	12/6/18			
	13/6/18		Battalion was relieved by the 2nd Bn. Welch Regt. moved back into billets in NOEUX-les-MINES.	H.S.
	14/6/18		Day spent in bathing & cleaning up.	
	15/6/18		Bn. carried out training in the HOUCHIN Area. A,B & D Coys practised the raid on a marked out course. C coy. carried out platoon tactical schemes & specialist training.	H.S.
	18/6/18			
	19/6/18		Bn. was due for a day in the country in the Bois D'Olhin Area, owing to heavy rain however this was cancelled & training was done in camp. Tactical schemes & specialist training in the Massingarbe Area. All Coys fired on the long Range. A gas projector demonstration was given to the Bde at 10 p.m. in the HOUCHIN Area.	H.S.
	20/6/18			H.S.

Army Form C. 2118.

WAR DIARY
or
INTELLIGENCE SUMMARY.
(Erase heading not required.)

Instructions regarding War Diaries and Intelligence Summaries are contained in F. S. Regs., Part II. and the Staff Manual respectively. Title pages will be prepared in manuscript.

Place	Date	Hour	Summary of Events and Information	Remarks and references to Appendices
Neoux-les-MINES	21/6/18		Relieved the 2nd R Sussex Regt. as support Bn. CAMBRIN Sector. Relief completed at 11.45 AM. "B" Coy attached to front line Bn.	DS
CAMBRIN	22/6/18 to 24/6/18		Very quiet time. Daily fatigues did not exceed 150 all ranks. Musketry, Gas Drill & Lewis Gun training was carried out by all coys.	DS
in the line	25/6/18		Bn. relieved 1st Bn. Cameron Highlanders on left Bn. CAMBRIN SECTOR. Company dispositions – B Coy – left front. A Coy – left support. C Coy – right support. D Coy – Right front. Relief complete at 6.15 PM.	DS
—do—	26/6/18 to 30/6/18		Very quiet tour. Enemy's artillery was very inactive, rarely replying to our harassing fire. The normal training laid down in the Bn. Trench Routine Orders was carried out i.e. Musketry, Gas drill and Lewis Gun instruction.	DS

D Dougha Stevenson Lt.

for. Captain & Adjutant.
1st Bn. Loyal N. Lancashire Regt.

1/LN Lawe R/1
Army Form C. 2118.

July 1918

CONFIDENTIAL

WAR DIARY
or
INTELLIGENCE SUMMARY.
(Erase heading not required.)

Place	Date	Hour	Summary of Events and Information	Remarks and references to Appendices
In the line	1/7/18 2/7/18		Very quiet days. Our artillery carried out the usual harrassing shoots. Hostile aircraft activity was normal	h28
	3/7/18		The Bn was relieved by the 1st CAMERON HIGHLANDERS during the afternoon. On relief A Coy moved back into the support Bn area in CAMBRIN. B Coy relieved the right support Coy of 1st The BLACK WATCH (right Bn) which moved back into Support Bn area to special training. D Coy relieved two platoons of The CAMERONS in reserve at PONT FIXE + 2 platoons in reserve in Lewis Keep & Maison Rouge. Bn HQ moved back into CAMBRIN CHATEAU. All moves completed without casualties at 7.30pm	h28
CAMBRIN	4/7/18 to		The two companies in CAMBRIN supplied an average of 200 men daily to work on the line. Those in reserve training daily was carried out in Musketry Gas Drill, Lewis Gun etc & special tactical training was done by all available officers NCOs under the C.O.	h28
	9/7/18		D Coy was relieved by C Coy on the 8th inst & B Coy by D Coy The BLACK WATCH on the 9th inst	h28

CONFIDENTIAL

Army Form C. 2118.

WAR DIARY
or
INTELLIGENCE SUMMARY.
(Erase heading not required.)

Instructions regarding War Diaries and Intelligence Summaries are contained in F. S. Regs., Part II. and the Staff Manual respectively. Title pages will be prepared in manuscript.

Place	Date	Hour	Summary of Events and Information	Remarks and references to Appendices
CAMBRIN	10/7/18		On the whole a quiet day. A few heavy shells fell in the Western End of the village between 9 & 9:30 AM. Two ORs were killed & one wounded. The usual working parties were found.	HDS
	11/7/18		Bn was relieved by the 2nd/4th The WELCH Regt. moved back into reserve billets in NOEUX-LES-MINES. Relief completed at 6.12.5 p.m. A.B. & Coys bathed in the afternoon.	BR
NOEUX LES MINES	12-21/7/18		Training during this period consisted mainly of the training of platoons in tactical schemes in the vicinity of NOEUX and at the Bois D'OHAIN. "A" "B" & "D" Coys carried out Coy MacLeans on the 11th 13th training areas on the 12th, 13th and 15th. On the 19th a route march via HOUCHIN, VAUDRICOURT, NOEUX LES MINES, HESDIGNEUL. On the 23rd battalion sports were held preparatory to Brigade Sports held on the 18th	R.A.D.E. R.A.D.E. R.A.D.E. R.A.D.E.

Army Form C. 2118.

CONFIDENTIAL

WAR DIARY
or
INTELLIGENCE SUMMARY.
(Erase heading not required.)

Instructions regarding War Diaries and Intelligence
Summaries are contained in F. S. Regs., Part II.
and the Staff Manual respectively. Title pages
will be prepared in manuscript.

Place	Date	Hour	Summary of Events and Information	Remarks and references to Appendices
	17/7/15		On the 17th we played the 6th LINCOLNS at football on our ground and beat them 3-1.	Ruse.
	20/7/15		On the 20th the 1st CAMERONS played us a return match on the BRAQUEMONT ground and beat us 1-3.	Ruse.
ANNEQUIN	21/7/15		The Battⁿ relieved the 1st NORTHAMPTONSHIRE REGT on the morning of the 21st at ANNEQUIN. Brig⁴⁹ being in the flag heads, A Coy in the Mine works B+D Coys in the village and C Coy in the VILLAGE LINE, all being support area.	Ruse.
	22/7/15 to 25/7/15		Whilst here two new huts start in autumn leaving leaving in between musketry and return in billets and a further two hours in the technical training of platoons in daylight patrolling. On the afternoon of the 25th the batt⁷ manned the defences of the ANNEQUIN locality for practice.	Ruse.
	26/7/15		The batt⁷ relieved the 1st Black Watch in the night two sector (left of VERMELLES) during the morning relievers of the 30th, B+D Coys	

CONFIDENTIAL

Army Form C. 2118.

WAR DIARY
or
INTELLIGENCE SUMMARY.
(Erase heading not required.)

Instructions regarding War Diaries and Intelligence Summaries are contained in F. S. Regs., Part II. and the Staff Manual respectively. Title pages will be prepared in manuscript.

Place	Date	Hour	Summary of Events and Information	Remarks and references to Appendices
			going to the left and right front company positions respectively. C. Coy in support in CENTRAL KEEP and A Coy in reserve. Bn HQS being in new dugouts being constructed just W of the VERMELLES - CAMBRIN road. The Black Watch took over the fire & support lines at ANNEQUIN, relief	R.H.D.E.
			was complete shortly before casualties by 5 p.m.	
In the Field	28/7/18		A quiet day. Our artillery active on enemy trenches and back areas. Usual cleaning of trenches and night wiring carried out.	R.H.D.E.
	28/7/18		Major Forrest 7th 2nd KRRC assumed command of the Batty vice Lt. Col. McPhillips DSO etc. to England for six months. Enemy were quiet save for a few light trench mortars. Our artillery carried out persistent harassing fire.	R.H.D.E.
	29/7/18		There was a fire in what should be enemy field guns on its reserve line of the front edge. Otherwise both our own and enemy artillery very quiet. The usual trench mortaring took place. Hostile aircraft activity practically nil.	R.H.D.E.

CONFIDENTIAL

Army Form C. 2118.

WAR DIARY
or
INTELLIGENCE SUMMARY.
(Erase heading not required.)

Instructions regarding War Diaries and Intelligence Summaries are contained in F. S. Regs., Part II. and the Staff Manual respectively. Title pages will be prepared in manuscript.

Place	Date	Hour	Summary of Events and Information	Remarks and references to Appendices
In the Field	30/8/18		There was the normal artillery activity. Enemy trench mortars carried out a destructive shoot on the RESERVE line in the afternoon.	R.N.W.
	31/8/18		On the whole a quiet day. The posts of B and A Coy in QUARRY ALLEY were shelled during the evening, but otherwise activity was normal.	R.N.W.
	26-31/8		The work during the period consisted mainly of all round defence wiring of the posts on the front. A large amount of trench repair was also effected and old useless trenches filled in or stopped. This we receive practically no harassing fire from the enemy.	
	1/9/18			R.N.W.

T.R. Rownd
Major
Comdg.
Comdg. of the 2/4th N. Lancashire Regt.

WAR DIARY
or
INTELLIGENCE SUMMARY.
(Erase heading not required.)

Army Form C.-2118.

August 1918

Place	Date	Hour	Summary of Events and Information	Remarks and references to Appendices
In line	1/8/18 to 9/8/18		Nothing of importance happened during the period. The enemy was very quiet & made very little retaliation to our harassing fire. Patrols were continually sent out but they were unable to engage the enemy. A divisional Horse Show was held near BRUAY on the 4th. The Bn obtained 1st in the 'Cross Country Race. Quarter mile, ½ mile & mile thrown out & also second in the Tug 'o' War.	R.A.O.E. R.N.O.E.
	10/8/18		Bn was relieved by 1st South Wales Borderers & we relief moved into reserve billets in NOEUX-les-MINES. Relief was completed without casualty at 11.40 AM. During the evening Noeux-le-Mines area were bombed but no casualties sustained.	R.N.O.E
NOEUX-les-MINES	11/8/18		About 9.15 AM the enemy commenced to shell the vicinity of the billets with H.V. guns of fairly large calibre. Men moved into the open country W. of the town. The shelling ceased at about 11.30 AM & Bn returned to billets. At 12.45 pm the shelling again started just as rations dinners were being issued. 27 casualties sustained. 5 killed & 22 wounded. The Bn moved into new billets	R.A.O.E R.N.O.E

WAR DIARY
or
INTELLIGENCE SUMMARY.
(Erase heading not required.)

Army Form C. 2118.

Place	Date	Hour	Summary of Events and Information	Remarks and references to Appendices
			area in the S. part of the town.	Ryn E
Noeux le Mines	12/8/18		The day was quiet. Bn housed in Bois D'OHLAIN. About 10.30 pm the town was lightly shelled by HV guns & Bn stood to in readiness to move. The shelling ceased at about 11.15 pm but restarted at 1.15 pm & Bn moved into open country W of the town returning to billets at 4.30 am. The shelling started again at 8.30 am. Bn immediately moved to the training area remained there until	
Camp K23 c+D	13/8/18 to 18/8/18		bivouac camp was prepared in K23 c+D (West of Noeux le Mines). Weather was very fine. Bns that the usual tactical training of platoons was carried out.	
PREDEFIN	19/8/18		Bn moved by Bus to billets in PREDEFIN about 8 miles west of PERNES	Rot E
	20/8/18		Day devoted to rest & general cleaning up	
	21/8/18 to 24/8/18		Four hours training carried out daily – Tactical training of platoons – Bayonet fighting – Lewis Gun training etc.	
	25/8/18		Sunday – no parades	Rtt NE
	26/8/18		Owing to heavy rain training was carried out in billets	Rtt NE

Army Form C. 2118.

WAR DIARY
~~INTELLIGENCE SUMMARY.~~
(Erase heading not required.)

Instructions regarding War Diaries and Intelligence Summaries are contained in F. S. Regs., Part II. and the Staff Manual respectively. Title pages will be prepared in manuscript.

Place	Date	Hour	Summary of Events and Information	Remarks and references to Appendices
PRÉDEFIN	27/8/18		A battalion scheme was carried out of advancing through open country to the attack on ground between HEUCHIN and PRÉDEFIN. Inter-company football matches in afternoon.	
	28/8/18		Company schemes carried out round village. Company Lewis Guns fired on 303 range. A rainy day.	R.M.N.E
	29/8/18		A brigade scheme carried out of an advance from EQUIRRE into high ground beyond PRÉDEFIN. Recreational training in afternoon.	R.M.A.E
	30/8/18		Company scheme (advance guard tactics and open warfare attack)	R.M.A.E
	31/8/18	4 p.m.	The Battn. left PRÉDEFIN, marched to ANVIN station, where they entrained 11 p.m. and arrived at ARRAS station 7.30 a.m. morning of 1st September.	R.M.A.E

2/8

Dawson
Major for Lieut. Col.
Commdg. 1st Bn. Loyal N. Lancashire Regt.

WAR DIARY

INTELLIGENCE SUMMARY.
(Erase heading not required.)

Army Form C. 2118.

September 1918

1/LN Lune R?

458 49

Place	Date	Hour	Summary of Events and Information	Remarks and references to Appendices
ARRAS.	1/9/18		On the night of the 31/1st, the Bn. marched up from RONVILLE CAVES ARRAS to assembly positions S.E of GUEMAPPE at 5am the barrage opened & at 10.45 the Bn. moved forward in artillery formation to consolidate the 1st objective (ridge running approximately N+S between the village of DURY the main ARRAS-CAMBRAI Rd) which the Canadians were reported to have taken. A+B Coys formed the front line — C coy support +D coy Reserve. The objective was reached about 1pm when it was found that the fight was still in progress. The Bn. accordingly withdrew about 200x & laid down in artillery formation under cover of the ridge. About 4pm orders were received to withdraw a further 1500x. This was done & the Bn. remained in these positions throughout the night. The casualties	
			sustained were very light – a number being caused by bombs & M.G. bullets from low flying aeroplanes.	W.B.S.
	2/9/18		During the morning reports were received that the enemy had retired over the SENSEE River & the CANAL DU NORD. During the afternoon the Bn. relieved the 4th division, who ...[torn]... outpost position	W.B.S.

WAR DIARY
or
INTELLIGENCE SUMMARY.
(Erase heading not required.)

Army Form C. 2118.

Instructions regarding War Diaries and Intelligence Summaries are contained in F. S. Regs., Part II. and the Staff Manual respectively. Title pages will be prepared in manuscript.

Place	Date	Hour	Summary of Events and Information	Remarks and references to Appendices
			North of the Canadians West of the SENSEE RIVER.	
DROCOURT – QUEANT LINE	3/9/18		The Bn. went into reserve in the DROCOURT – QUEANT LINE – The Black Watch being in the front line. The Canadians in support. Relief completed about 8.15 p.m.	WS.
	to		Very little of importance happened during the period. On the night of the 3rd, a bomb was dropped on D Coy's ration party causing 14 casualties. CQMS Stanway + Sgt Watson late. died from wounds received on this occasion.	WS.
	7/9/18			
"Y" HUTS W. of ARRAS.	6/9/18		Bn. was relieved by the 1st Q.W.R. Moved out by march route + route to "Y" Huts, about 10 Kilometre West of ARRAS, arriving about 9.30 p.m. 3 casualties were sustained during the relief. Total casualties during period 1 – 8/9/18 – Killed 12 ORs. Wounded 107 ORs. Gassed 9 ORs. Missing 1 OR.	WS.
–do–	9/9/18		Day spent in cleaning up + preparation for move on the 10th.	WS.
	10/9/18		Bn. complete with transport, entrained at MARCEUIL Stn. about 12 noon + moved via DOULLENS to MARCELCAVE (about 9 miles S.E. of AMIENS) arriving about 1 AM 11th inst.	WS.

Army Form C. 2118.

WAR DIARY
or
INTELLIGENCE SUMMARY.
(Erase heading not required.)

Instructions regarding War Diaries and Intelligence Summaries are contained in F. S. Regs., Part II. and the Staff Manual respectively. Title pages will be prepared in manuscript.

Place	Date	Hour	Summary of Events and Information	Remarks and references to Appendices
MORCOURT	11/9/18		Bn detrained at MARCELCAVE about 1AM marched to MORCOURT. Coys were billeted in shelters in a bank on the East side of the village - HQ in the village.	
-do-	12/9/18		Day devoted to rest & cleaning up. Transport moved by road to area near BRIE.	WS
ESTRÉES	13/9/18		Bn moved by bus to bivouacs in the vicinity of ESTRÉES arriving about 12 noon.	WS
POEUILLY	14/9/18		Bn marched to bivouacs ½ mile south of POEUILLY arriving about 11AM.	WS
VERMAND	15/9/18		Bn marched to bivouacs in Vermand arriving about 6pm.	WS
In the line	16/9/18		The Bn relieved the 15th Bn the Gloucester Regt in the line on the night of the 16th. Sectors	WS
-do-	17/9/18		On the morning of the 17th. in conjunction with operations carried out by the right hand Division the Bn front was straightened by the right coy establishing a post on the high ground in M.25.c.	WS
-do-	18/9/18		At 5.30 AM the Bn attacked in conjunction with troops on the right & left. Details of the fight are shown in the "Report on Operations 17/9/18 to 24/9/18" attached. The Bn remained in the positions gained on the 18th - nothing of importance happening during the day	WS WS

Army Form C.2118.

WAR DIARY
or
INTELLIGENCE SUMMARY

September 1918

(Erase heading not required.)

Place	Date	Hour	Summary of Events and Information	Remarks and references to Appendices
Outpost line	20/9/18		After dusk the one company in the front line was withdrawn about 700 x West and replaced by a company of the 15th Black Watch.	
"	21/9/18		Relieved 15th The Cameron Highlanders as Left Bn of the Bde — A & B Coys taking over the front line, with C & D Coys in support	
"	22/9/18		The day passed quietly. About 6.30pm the enemy after barrage fire attempted to occupy a portion of GALLICHET trench, held by the 1/5 Sherwood Foresters. The attempt was repulsed with the assistance of B' Coy who opened fire from the flank with rifle & Lewis Guns.	
"	23/9/18 & 24/9/18		On the night of the 23/24 the whole Bde formed up in rear of the front line held by this Bn. At 3AM the support coys went withdrawn & at 4.30AM the two front coys withdrew — the whole Bn marching back to bivouacs in CAULAINCOURT WOOD near VERMAND. In spite of very heavy harassing fire no casualties were sustained in this move.	
	25/9/18		Day devoted to rest & reorganisation	
	26/9/18		The Bn relieved two companies of the 1st Sherwood Foresters & 2 coys of the 5th Lincolns as Left Bn of the Bde — the line running N of the village of PONTRUET	

WAR DIARY
or
INTELLIGENCE-SUMMARY.

(Erase heading not required.)

September 1918

Army Form C. 2118.

Place	Date	Hour	Summary of Events and Information	Remarks and references to Appendices
In the field	27/9/18		Quiet day	WS
"	28/9/18		Quiet day. At 11.30 pm Bn HQ moved forward & established HQ in the left front coy line	WS
"	29/9/18		In conjunction with operations of the 4th Division on the left, the Bn moved forward at 5.50 AM & formed a defensive flank on the Western Bank of the St. QUENTIN CANAL. The operation was successfully carried out in a dense fog. 250 prisoners were captured & 35 machine guns. Our casualties were very light. Full details of the operation are given in the "Summary of operations 25th to 4th October" (attached.) At 5 pm the Bn withdrawn into Bde reserve & occupied trenches area North of the road between BERTAUCOURT & PONTRUET, remaining there through the night.	WS
"	30/9/18		The Bn moved forward at 2 pm to relieve the 1st Dorsets North of the Canal as left Bn of the Bde - resting in the canal tunnel just East of LEHAUCOURT until dark. The relief was completed about 5.30 AM on the 1st October.	WS

Army Form C. 2118.

WAR DIARY
or
INTELLIGENCE SUMMARY.

(Erase heading not required.)

September 1918.

Place	Date	Hour	Summary of Events and Information	Remarks and references to Appendices
			Total casualties during the month	
			Officers - Killed 3. Other Ranks - Killed 42	
			Wounded 12. Wounded 200.	
			Missing 1. Missing 17	
			Two Officers & 300 ORs were captured & 45 Machine Guns taken	
			Approximately 4 Officers & 150 ORs joined during the month.	WR
			Douglas Stephenson Capt.	
			1st/Col. Cmdg 1st N. Lancs. Regt.	
	8/10/18			

SECRET

WAR DIARY
or
INTELLIGENCE SUMMARY
(Erase heading not required.)

Army Form C. 2118.

October 1918

1 L.N. Lancs

Place	Date	Hour	Summary of Events and Information	Remarks and references to Appendices
In line	1/10/18		Reld of 15th Doset completed about 5.30AM (see War Diary for previous month) Day passed quietly	W.S.
"	2/10/18		Advance of the 9th Corps continued. But took to prevent any gap between the Left division & the French on the right. Coys advanced in artillery formation at ZERO (8.30AM) in oder C.D.A.B. C company leading Coy immediately gained touch with the Left division. The French were unable to move forward & Lewis with them were not established with them. The advance of the Left division was held up at the village of SEQUEHART, the Bn took up a line running from H.35.a.63 to N.4.a.7.2. Conference Map Thorigny (..) in Lewis with Left & right divisions. About 6.30pm the troops of Left division holding SEQUEHART were heavily counter attacked & forced to withdraw to a line on the N edge of the village. The line held by the Bn was heavily shelled during this counter attack & some 50 casualties were sustained	
"	3/10/18		Previous dispositions were continued at ZERO 6.35AM, coys moving forward in arial formation & order. About 7.45AM the enemy about 250	W.S.

WAR DIARY
or
INTELLIGENCE SUMMARY.
(Erase heading not required.)

Army Form C. 2118.

Place	Date	Hour	Summary of Events and Information	Remarks and references to Appendices
			Strong accompanied by light machine guns, debouched from CARISE WOOD sundu cover of heavy machine gun fire attempted to work round the village of SEQUEHART from the South. The troops of the left division in SEQUEHART withdrew. C.D. 4A Coys formed a defensive flank on the high ground in H.35.b, met the enemy repulsed him at the point of the bayonet. The general advance not being continued, the companies re-organised & took up the positions held at Zero. The Bn was relieved during the night by 1/5 The Black Watch & moved to the Canal Tunnel in FLECHE WOOD. Casualties during the period 1st - 3rd (inclusive) approximately 8 officers & 200 O.Rs.	
South of LEHAUCOURT	4/10/18		At 9.30 a.m. the Bn moved back into bivouacs in the trench area S. of the Canal just S. of LEHAUCOURT.	
VERMAND	5/10/18		Leaving bivouac area at 8.30 A.M., the Bn moved back by march route to bivouacs in CAULAINCOURT WOOD near VERMAND.	

Army Form C. 2118.

WAR DIARY
or
INTELLIGENCE SUMMARY.
(Erase heading not required.)

Instructions regarding War Diaries and Intelligence Summaries are contained in F. S. Regs., Part II. and the Staff Manual respectively. Title pages will be prepared in manuscript.

Place	Date	Hour	Summary of Events and Information	Remarks and references to Appendices
VERMAND	6/10/18 to 8/10/18		The Battalion rested and reformed. The training of Lewis Gunners and signallers being especially attend to.	Iys
N.W. of BELLENGLISE	9/10/18		Took over area and billets in trench system. Reforming and training carried out.	Iys
	10/10/18 to 11/10/18		Lt. Col. Berkeley D.S.O took over command. Bad weather hindered training	
	12/10/18 to 15/10/18		Training was carried on during this period	Iys
BOHAIN.	16/10/18.		The Battalion received orders to proceed to a forward area and made to m ~~france~~ BOHAIN doing a march of 15 miles. Bn moved off from billets at 0700 hrs and arrived at BOHAIN at 1500 hrs. Quarters having been received for the following day a reconnaissance was made by the Company Commanders. The rest of the Battalion remained in billets at BOHAIN.	Iys

Army Form C. 2118.

WAR DIARY
or
INTELLIGENCE SUMMARY.
(Erase heading not required.)

Instructions regarding War Diaries and Intelligence Summaries are contained in F. S. Regs, Part II. and the Staff Manual respectively. Title pages will be prepared in manuscript.

Place	Date	Hour	Summary of Events and Information	Remarks and references to Appendices
SE of BECQUIGNY	17/10/18		Reference ANDIGNY FOREST (5ySE a 62 BNE). Operation orders having been received the Battalion moved from Billets in BOHAIN to assembly positions SE of BECQUIGNY D 6 b. The IX Corps was ordered to attack and take three objectives viz the Red Dotted, Red and Green lines respectively. The first task being allotted to the 6th Division and the 2nd and 3rd to the 1st Division. The remaining Division the 46th to attack on the Right of the 1st Division. On the left of the Corps front two American divisions were operating and on the Right the French. At 0520 hrs the Battn moved forward in a very thick mist on the Right of the CAMBRAI Highlanders and struck the VAUX ANDIGNY - LES FERMES Road at BELLE-VUE. The enemy were in a strong position North of BELLE-VUE and the Cameron suffered heavily on arrival onto the top of the Ridge at the Shrine of BELLE-VUE. Two Companies and Battn HQ moved round the flanks of a large number of the enemy (Number 170 approx). Our casualties there were 1 Officer and 15 OR wounded. These two Companies were	

Army Form C. 2118.

WAR DIARY
or
INTELLIGENCE SUMMARY.
(Erase heading not required.)

Instructions regarding War Diaries and Intelligence Summaries are contained in F. S. Regs., Part II. and the Staff Manual respectively. Title pages will be prepared in manuscript.

Place	Date	Hour	Summary of Events and Information	Remarks and references to Appendices
			Then reformed and moved on LES GOBELETS which was found to be occupied. ANDIGNY-LES-FERMES was evidently occupied by the enemy as fire was coming from this front. These two companies then advanced under very heavy fire and captured the village taking about 70 prisoners. Casualties in ANDIGNY-LES-FERMES being 5 killed and five wounded. These Companies were relieved during the afternoon by Companies from another division and on its withdrawal to Battery the others moving to the SUNKEN ROAD NE of ANDIGNY LES FERMES. The two Companies which had lost touch will now be dealt with. D Coy advanced approximately in the correct direction and struck the VAUX - ANDIGNY - ANDIGNY LES FERMES Road between LES GOBELETS and ANDIGNY-LES-FERMES, NORTH of the MILL and advanced to the SUNKEN ROAD running NORTH EAST. "A" Company after crossing the REGNICOURT Road moved in the direction of the orchard West of ANDIGNY-LES-FERMES. At about 0830 hrs the mist suddenly cleared, and the enemy opened heavy fire with	

WAR DIARY
or
INTELLIGENCE SUMMARY.
(Erase heading not required.)

Army Form C. 2118.

Place	Date	Hour	Summary of Events and Information	Remarks and references to Appendices
			two field guns and two machine guns were rushed and captured. The guns were then rushed and captured. Casualties from these guns Casualties from these guns which were firing at point blank range hav[ing] four killed and four wounded. This Company then moved North of ANDIGNY-LES-FERME and occupied a sunken road already occupied by "D" Coy. The Battalion then had Three Companies Trying to work forward towards the BLANCS FOSSES road and one in reserve at LES GOBELETS. On trying to work forward to BLANCS FOSSE these Companies came under very heavy machine gun fire and about 1645 the enemy opened a heavy HE and gas barrage and these Companies suffered several casualties from this barrage. The Batt. then dug in for the night. The whole operations during the day were most successful.	JyS
	18/10/18		The Battalion was relieved in the front line by the 6th Leicestershire Regt and proceeded to the area around BELLE-VUE	

Army Form C. 2118.

WAR DIARY
or
INTELLIGENCE SUMMARY.
(Erase heading not required.)

Place	Date	Hour	Summary of Events and Information	Remarks and references to Appendices
	18/10/18.		The Battalion was to in Brigade Reserve and as an attack was being made by the 1st Black Watch and the 1st Cameron Highlanders the Battalion moved up to ANGIN FARM in readiness to support either Battalion. As they were not called upon they remained there until 21.00 hrs when two Companies and Battalion Hq moved up to MAL ASSISE FARM and spent the night there	
LA VALLÉE MULATRE	19/10/18		The Battalion moved back to billets in LA VALLÉE MULATRE	
	20/10/18.		Reorgd and cleaned up.	
BUSIGNY WASSIGNY	23/10/18		The Battalion moved up to WASSIGNY a village about 3 Kilos from the line.	
	24/10/18		Relieved the 2nd Welsh and 1st Gloucesters taking up a front of nearly 4000 yds just in front of the OISE CANAL. Three Companies were in the line and on in Support. On the right were the French with an intermediate post between divisions and on the left the Black Watch who held the outskirts of the village of CATILLON. Relief was carried out quite well inspite of the	

Place	Date	Hour	Summary of Events and Information	Remarks and references to Appendices
	25/10/18		different nature of the country which was split up into many small fields with formidable hedges separating them.	
	26/10/18		The enemy opposite us were very active and during the night crowd the canal and patrolled new to our lines. Enemy artillery was very active and shelled continuously night and day. Enemy's artillery fire quietened down but machine guns were still active firing from the East bank of the Canal. A few evacuations were made by gas. The enemy apparently captured one of our men during a patrol encounter in which no enemy casualties were sustained from machine gun fire was killed a few directed from the same lane.	
	27/10/18		Enemy continued to patrol the West side of the Canal and a party of 15 having approached one of our posts was fired on and withdrew with loss. The Battalion was relieved in the evening by the 2 KRRC and 1st Northampton -shire Regt.	

Army Form C. 2118.

WAR DIARY
or
INTELLIGENCE SUMMARY.
(Erase heading not required.)

Instructions regarding War Diaries and Intelligence Summaries are contained in F. S. Regs., Part II. and the Staff Manual respectively. Title pages will be prepared in manuscript.

Place	Date	Hour	Summary of Events and Information	Remarks and references to Appendices
	27/10/18	(cont)	Relieve was completed satisfactorily and the Battalion moved back to billets in WASSIGNY.	
WASSIGNY	28/10/18		The Battalion rested and cleaned up. A draft of 181 was received and there were spot up amongst the four companies. The enemy directed a certain amount of shelling against the billets and 3 O.R. were killed and 13 wounded.	Fys
	29/10/18		Reorganization of coys was carried out. At about 18.00 hrs the SOS was reported from the Left Battalion front and C & D coys immediately moved up into support. No action developed.	Fys
	30/10/18		The two Companies returned during had down casualties, Reorganisation was carried out amongst the two Companies and a certain amount of training carried out	Fys

R.U.Barkley Lt. Colonel
Comdg 1/4 yal Lancashire Regt

2/11/18

Headquarters
1st Brigade.

Reference Maps 62c SE. and 62b AM S.W. 1/20000.
Report on Operations 17/9/18 to 24/9/18.

Night 16/17th. The Battalion relieved the 1st Battn Gloster Regt in line on right of the Brigade Sector.

17th On the morning of the 17th in conjunction with operations carried out by the Division on the right flank, the Battalion front was straightened by the right Company establishing a post on the high ground in M.25.c.

18th. By 4.45am the Battalion was formed up on the jumping off line,preparatory to attack.
    "C" Coy. Left Front Company
    "D" " Right Front Company
    "A" " Support Company
    "B" " Reserve Company.

At 5.30 am the Battalion advanced to the attack in a thick mist and rain . No land Marks were visible.
Battalion Headquarters moved forward at ZERO and was established at M.25.c/2 4.8..
First objective should have been reached by 6.24 am.
Right Company reported objective obtained.
Left Company reported that it was held up by very heavy machine Gun fire in the Valley in M.20.
An officers patrol and scouts were sent out to endeavour to locate the position of the Right Front and Support Companies, but were unsuccessful in doing so.
The Reserve Company (B) Coy) was sent up at 8 am. to enter first objective on the left of the Left Front Company,which,as stated,was held up in M.20.d. and to establish touch with right Front Company, and with it to continue the advance to 2nd objective. Left Front Company (C Coy.) was ordered to move forward in reserve.
Resevre Company (B Coy) entered the Forst Obje ctive VILLEMAY TRENCH about M.20. b.7.6.and secured the Battalions First Objective.
Right being M.21.c.8.5. The Enemy immediately counter attacked, debouching from ARBOUSIERS WOOD and an unnamed wood in M.21.a. under cover from heavy machine gun fire from high kround in M.21.d. which compled completly enfiladed the position held by the Company and they were forced to give ground in spite of making a strong resistance , during which the Company Commander Capt.R.M.Leake M.C. was killed.
The company was again led to the attack and re-established itself but was unable to hold the whole of the position.

D.Coy, the right front company was located in M.27.a. and C with the Support Company (A.Coy.) in close proximity , As soon as their positions were ascertained, they were withdrawn.
D Coy into support and A Coy was ordered to fill position of the Right Front Company but was unable owing to Machine Gun Fire to enter VILLEMAY TRENCH.
At dark C.Coy. whi had been held up in M.20.d was ordered to enter VILLEMAY TRENCH and prolong the line from B Coyany Right, whcih rested about M.20.b.7.3. to M.21.C.8.5.
This was carried out , but it was foind impossible to hold this position owing to the very havy Machine Gun Fire, which completely enfiladed the position. The Company had to be withdrawn with its right on a point M.20.b.

During the night September 18/19th the Battalion took up a position to form a defesive flank in the high ground in M.26 a. and c.

In spite of the leading Companies each having an officer marching on a Compass Bearing in their outer flanks, both companies lost their directions, the left Company but slightly, which was due to heavy enfilade Machine Gun Fire down the valley in M.20.c and d.

The Right Front Company came under Machine Gun Fire almost immediately the advance commenced and met with slight resistance from Woods in M.26.d. which diverted the line of march of the Compass party, this and feeling for the right Division on the right, I attribute to be the cause of the right Companiy's loss of direction, they were unable to recover their direction owing to no land marks being visible in the mist added to which, they were drawn by Machine Gun Fire from ythe Right Flank, on reaching what they assumed to be their 1st objective the Company Commander Lieut. CSandalls was reported missing.

When the mist lifted this Company and A Company the support company found themselves in a position in M.27.a and c. which was under very heavy Machine Gun Fire and it was inly possible to withdraw these Companies, a very few at a time, which necessitated a long operation.

The wide frontage of 500 yards per Company made it extremely difficulty under the most trying circumstances to keep touch and direction, every effort was made to do so, by means of compass patrols and scouts.

The advance beyond the Forst Objective was impossibleowing to the fact that ARBOUSIERS WOOD and FRESNOY LE PETIT held out.

Night 21st. The battalion relieved the 1st Bn. Cameron Highlanders as left Battalion of the Brigade.

Night 22nd. About 8.30 pm the enemy after a barrage attempted to capture GALLCHET TRENCH held by the 5th Sherwood Foresters. This attack was repulsed with the aid of our left Company B Coy who opened fire rifles and Lewis Gun as the enemy advanced.

Night 23/24th. Wnd Brigade assembled in the area just rear of front line held by the Battalion. B.D. and 2 platoons of A Coy were withdrawn at 3.30am the 24th. Remaining platoons of A.Coy and C.Coy. were withdrawn at R.E 4.30 am. The whole battalion moving back into bivouac in CAULAINCOURT WOOD.

Casulalties during this period as under:-
    OFFICERS   Killed   2.
                Wounded   7
                Missing   1.
    Other Ranks Killed   48
                Wounded 180
                Missing   9
                Gassed   21 (Not yet diagnosed).

Lt.Colonel,
Comdg. 1st Bn.Loyal North Lancs Regt.

6/10/18.

SECRET

NARRATIVE OF OPERATIONS OF 1st DIVISION
ON SEPTEMBER 18th AND 19th, 1918.

(a). ORDER OF BATTLE.

    G.O.C. Major-General E.P. STRICKLAND, C.B., C.M.G., D.S.O.

    1st Inf. Bde.
        Brigadier-General W.B. THORNTON, D.S.O.

        1st Bn. The Black Watch (Royal Highlanders).
        1st Bn. The Loyal North Lancashire Regt).
        1st Bn. Queens Own Cameron Highlanders.
        1st Trench Mortar Battery.

      Attached.
        "A" Coy. 1st Bn. Machine Gun Corps.
        1 Section 23rd Field Coy. R.E.

    2nd Inf. Bde.
        Brigadier-General G.C. KELLY.

        2nd Bn. The Royal Sussex Regt.
        1st Bn. The Northamptonshire Regt.
        2nd Bn. The King's Royal Rifle Corps.
        2nd Trench Mortar Battery.

      Attached.
        "B" Coy. 1st Bn. Machine Gun Corps.
        409th Field Coy. R.E.

    Artillery.
        C.R.A. Brigadier-General H.F.E. LEWIN, C.M.G.

        25th Bde. R.F.A. } 1st Divl. Artillery.
        39th Bde. R.F.A.

      Attached.
        5th Army Bde. R.H.A.
        16th Army Bde. R.H.A.
        168th Bde. R.F.A. (32nd Divl. Artillery).
        298th Army Bde. R.F.A.
        14th Bde. R.G.A.

    In Reserve.
        3rd Inf. Bde.
        1st Bn. Machine Gun Corps less "A" & "B" Coys.
        23rd Field Coy. R.E. (less 1 Section).
        26th Field Coy. R.E.
        1/6th Bn. The Welch Regt. (Pioneers).

(b). DISPOSITIONS.

Detailed dispositions of troops at Zero are shewn on Map attached.

Headquarters.

Adv. Div. H.Q.   — CAULAINCOURT.   W.5.a.4.7.

Rear Div. H.Q.   — MERAUCOURT.   V.12.b.6.7.

D.A.   — CAULAINCOURT.   W.5.a.4.6.

Right Group R.F.A. — R.31.d.3.6.

Left Group R.F.A. — VERMAND.

D.E.   — CAULAINCOURT.   W.5.a.3.8.

Field Coys. R.E. less 409th Field Coy. R.E. and 1 Section 23rd Field Coy. R.E. and Pioneers concentrated in area around VERMAND.

Right Bde.   — 1st Inf. Bde. H.Q. R.32.b.1.2.

Left Bde.   — 2nd Inf. Bde. H.Q. R.32.b.1.2.

Reserve Bde   — 3rd Inf. Bde. H.Q. W.5.a.4.7.

troops in CAULAINCOURT - VERMAND Area.

* *

(3).

(c). BRIEF PLAN OF THE OPERATIONS.

IX Corps on right of Fourth Army had been driving the enemy rearguards back on to the main HINDENBURG LINE of Defences. By the evening of the 13th the resistance of the enemy rearguards had become such as to necessitate a major operation. Fourth Army decided to attack on its whole front on the 18th with the co-operation of a French Corps on its right: the IX Corps on the right and Australian Corps next it on the left. IX Corps was to attack on a two Division front 6th Div. on the right, 1st Division on the left. 4th Australian Division was on the left of the 1st Division.

General outline of the plan was communicated to Divisional Commander on the afternoon of the 13th instant and following days were spent in preparation. 3rd Inf. Bde. remained as advance guard on the Divisional front until night 16/17th when the attacking Inf. Bdes. (1st and 2nd Inf. Bdes) went into the line. Attached map shews Divisional and Inter-Bde. boundaries, objectives (GREEN, RED and BLUE) and the Infantry forming up line also the position of attacking Inf. Bdes. at Zero hour.

The Infantry forming up line was laid down by the Army to make a straight barrage along the Army front. Before the actual operation took place the advance guard Bde. had made progress on practically the whole Divisional front beyond the line laid down. To conform with our neighbours the right Bn. of the 1st Inf. Bde. and the left Bn. of the 2nd Inf. Bde. withdrew to the starting off line before Zero. In the centre, however, opposite MAISSEMY on the front of the two centre Bns. the forming up line was advanced 600 yards. The creeping barrage when it came down in front of these Bns., waited for the creeping barrage on the flanks to come up in line when the whole rolled forward together.

General Plan.

The GREEN and RED objectives were to be gained under creeping barrage; there was to be a halt of 2 hours on the GREEN objective. After reaching the RED objective Inf. Bdes. were to consolidate: the protective barrage lifting after 15 minutes. Exploitation if possible was to commence 2 hours after arrival at RED Line. During these 2 hours arrangements were made for Heavy Artillery to bombard selected points in the enemy's defences in front.

Artillery Plan.

All Artillery of the IX Corps was under the C.R.A., IX Corps for the operation. The C.R.A., 1st Division controlled the 6 Bdes. of Field and Horse Artillery operating on the 1st Division front and also had a direct call on 1 Bde. of Heavy Artillery (3 - 6" Hows. Batteries). All Field Artillery was sited so as to be able to fire a barrage up to the RED Line inclusive without moving. For purposes of exploitation the 25th and 39th Bdes. R.F.A. of 1st Divisional Artillery were to move forward after the capture of the RED Line each Bde. coming directly under the orders of one of the attacking Inf. Bdes.

The 18-pdr. barrage was to come down 200 yards in front of the Infantry forming up line at Zero. The 4.5" How. barrage was to come down 200 yards beyond the 18-pdr. barrage.

Artillery lifts were to be 100 yards.
    1st lift to be at Zero plus 3 minutes.
    2nd lift to be at Zero plus 5 minutes.
    3rd to 11th lift (both inclusive) lifts to be at 3 minutes interval.
    From 12th lift (inclusive) all lifts would be at 4 minutes interval.

/ Machine Guns..........

(4).

Machine Guns.

In addition to 1 M.G. Coy. co-operating directly with each Inf.
Bde. a further Coy. was organised by O.C. M.G.Bn. into 2 Sub-Groups
each of 8 guns which assembled at Zero 2,500 yards behind the jumping
off line. One of these Sub-Groups was to advance in each Inf. Bde.
area starting at Zero plus 3½ hours with the object of taking up
positions between the GREEN and RED objectives with a view to adding
depth to the defences when the RED Line was gained and to be able
to direct long range harassing fire beyond the BLUE Line.

Zero hour was to be at 5.30 a.m. (British Summer Time).

N.B.- Sun rose at 6.27 a.m.

(6). ACCOUNT OF THE ACTION.

Commencement of the action went according to plan. The
Zero hour was found to be too early and it was very difficult to
see. The right Bn. of the 1st Inf. Bde. appears to have lost
direction and to have been diverted towards FRESNOY where the attack
of the 6th Div. on our right was shortly held up. The general course
of the action on the 1st Division front was largely influenced by
the action of our neighbours. On the left the 4th Australian Division
carried everything before them, the 119th German Division surren-
dering freely and fighting badly; the Australians reached their
RED objective with little difficulty and on night 18/19th exploited
forward to the trenches in prolongation of 1st Division BLUE Line.
On their immediate right the 2nd Royal Sussex Regt. equally carried
everything before them and reached their RED Line but according
to orders did not exploit until 2 hours later. Owing to the events
on their right this Bn. had however, suffered considerable
casualties and were unable to exploit without further Artillery
preparation which was arranged by the Bde. that evening at 12
midnight when this Bn. established itself on the YELLOW Line marked
on Map. Omitting the 2nd K.R.R.Corps on the right of the 2nd Inf.
Bde. it is necessary to turn to the action of the 1st Inf. Bde. Here
the 79th German Division fought well both against this Bde. and
against the 6th Div. The latter who had considerable difficulties
in forming up never got really going on their right with the result
that they were unable to storm FRESNOY which was very strongly held.
North of the German positions at FRESNOY there was an open Valley,
the slopes of which were studded with Machine Guns in ARBOUSIERS
WOOD, CORMOUILLERS WOOD, MARRONNIERS WOOD. No one could advance up
the Valley without capturing or neutralizing FRESNOY and the high
ground North of ARBOUSIERS WOOD. Movement on the high ground North
of ARBOUSIERS WOOD was also enfiladed from the FRESNOY position. The
Loyal North Lancs. on the right were soon held up in the mouth of
the Valley, got mixed up with the 6th Div. troops opposite FRESNOY
and made no further progress. On their left, the 1st Cameron
Highlanders were delayed by the failure on the right, lost the
barrage and had to fight their way into the VILLEMAY TRENCH on
their GREEN objective where they found uncut wire.

In spite of this the left Coy. secured the objective and
after some bomb fighting this Bn. captured all GREEN Line and succeeded in advancing to time to its RED objective irrespective of the
difficulties on the flank. Its extreme left practically reached
the RED Line but by that time its flank was completely in the air
and the enemy was sending fresh troops up FOURMOY and ESSLING ALLEYS.
The Bn. threw a flank back to join up with the 1st Loyal North Lancs
and eventually took up the position shewn on the YELLOW Line on Map.

Returning to the right Bn. of the 2nd Inf. Bde. (2nd
K.R.R.Corps). This Bn. had to work up the OMIGNON Valley keeping
touch with the 2nd Royal Sussex across the Valley.

/ It succeeded......

It succeeded admirably in its task though it had to fight its way forward with its own covering fire as the nature of the ground and the obstacles prevented it keeping up with the barrage between the BLUE and RED objectives especially in BERTHAUCOURT.

The above represents the progress of the Battle generally. Reports received at Advanced Divl. H.Q. from various sources during the fighting were sufficient to indicate quite clearly the general trend of what was happening and in confirmation of telephone instructions to Inf. Bdes. a message was sent by Divl. H.Q. to Bdes. at 12.11 p.m. pointing out that the left had made progress and resistance appeared to decrease on the North and increase on the South. Bdes. to exploit this by using their Reserves on their left.

As a matter of fact the 1st Inf. Bde. were unable to employ their support Bn. as they had not brought it up soon enough. The 2nd Inf. Bde. did not need their support Bn. except for the exploitation which was carried out at 12 midnight and the Brigadier rightly decided then that he would use the tired Bn. which knew the ground rather than employ another Bn. in the dark which though fresh did not know the ground so well.

During the night Inf. Bdes. held the YELLOW Line shewn on map, 1st Inf. Bde. being directed to work up to RED Line North of ESSLING ALLEY as early as possible.

On the 19th 1st Inf. Bde. attempted at 9 a.m. with 2 Coys of 1st Black Watch to advance North of ESSLING ALLEY. Owing to Machine Gun fire from FRESNOY direction movement was practically confined to trenches and soon became apparent that nothing but a further organised attack would enable the Bde. to reach the SAMPSON and CHEVILLARD Trench System.

During this day there was stiff trench fighting in FOURNOY and ESSLING ALLEYS and East of BETHAUCOURT, the enemy infiltrating up these trenches and especially up the Sunken Road and Valley 600 yards S.E. of BERTHAUCOURT. It was obvious in these circumstances that no progress of any value could be made unless FRESNOY was captured at the same time. Bdes. were instructed to consolidate.

The situation was reported to the Corps and plans were commenced for further operations which took place on the 24th.

Casualties incurred during these operations were :-
    Killed - 15 Officers, 171 Other Ranks.
    Wounded - 22 Officers, 709 Other Ranks.
    Missing - 2 Officers, 37 Other Ranks.

Prisoners and material captured were :-
    Prisoners (Unwounded - 8 Officers, 311 Other Ranks.
          (Wounded - 3 Officers, 63 Other Ranks.

    Material - 9 - 77 mm. Field Guns.
             4 H.T.Ms.
             7 L.T.Ms.
             Many Machine Guns. (Total not counted).

* * *

W.O 95
1266

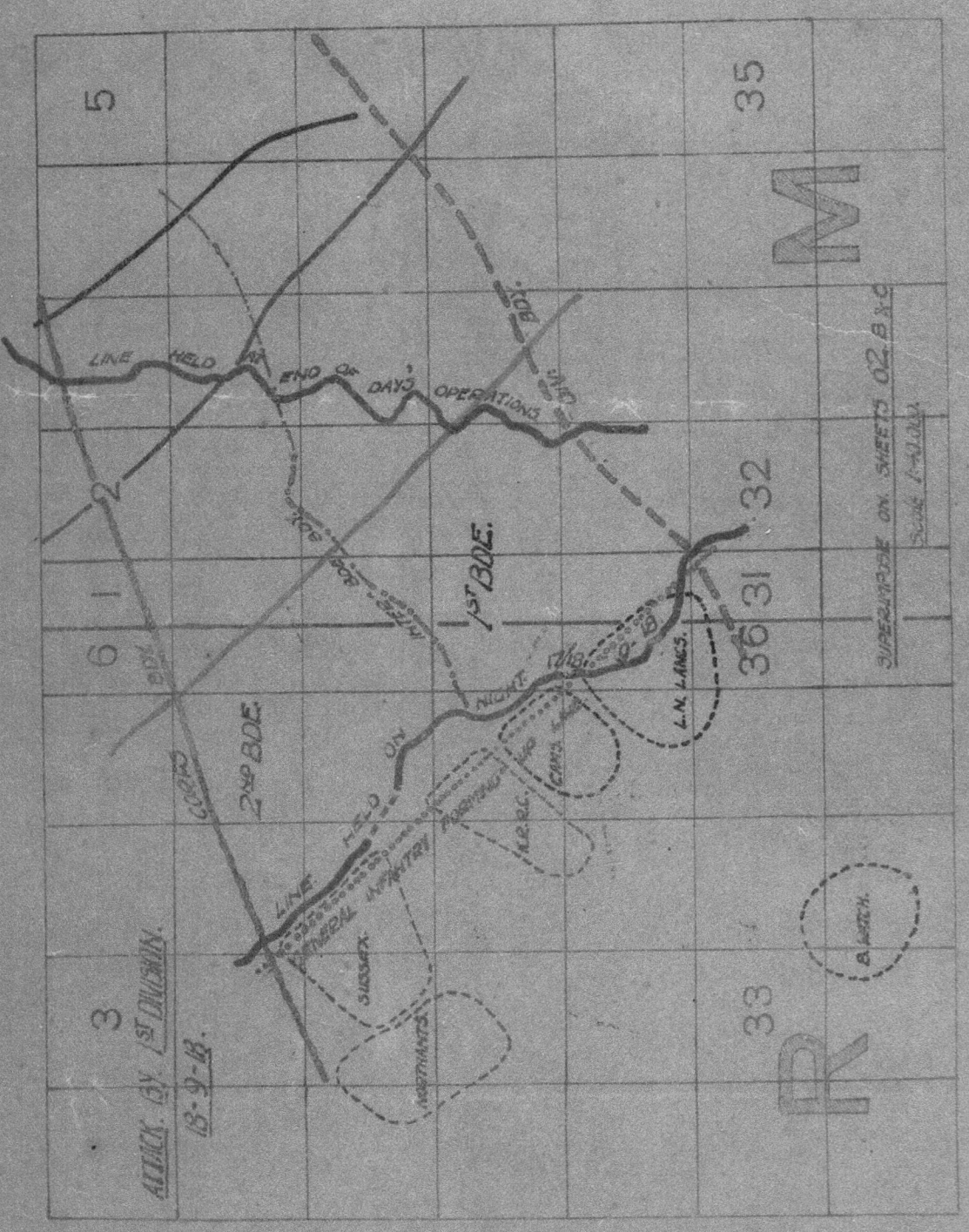

SECRET

This is a S E C R E T Document.

No copies are to be made.

The recipient is responsible that the instructions contained in D.R.O. No. 936 dated 21/10/18 are complied with.

* *

2nd Bn. The Royal Sussex Regt.
1st Bn. The Northamptonshire Regt.
2nd Bn. The King's Royal Rifle Corps.
2nd Trench Mortar Battery.

Attached.
"B" Coy. 1st Bn. Machine Gun Corps.
1 Section 23rd Field Coy. R.E.
Nos. 4 and 5 Sections "C" Coy. 13th Bn. Tank Corps.

3rd Inf. Bde.
Brigadier-General Sir W.A.I.KAY, Bt., C.M.G., D.S.O.

1st Bn. The South Wales Borderers.
1st Bn. The Gloucestershire Regt.
2nd Bn. The Welch Regt.
3rd Trench Mortar Battery.

Attached.
"C" Coy. 1st Bn. Machine Gun Corps.
2 Sections "D" Coy. 1st Bn. Machine Gun Corps.
1 Section 26th Field Coy. R.E.
No.3. Section "C" Coy. 13th Bn. Tank Corps.

Operating on Right Bde. front for Smoke Barrage :-
No.1. Special Coy. R.E. (Mortar).

Artillery.
C.R.A. Brigadier-General H.F.E. LEWIN, C.M.G.

25th Bde. R.F.A.) 1st Divl. Artillery.
39th Bde. R.F.A.)

Attached.
5th Army Bde. R.H.A.
16th Army Bde. R.H.A.
168th Bde. R.F.A. (32nd Divl. Artillery).
298th Army Bde. R.F.A.
14th Bde. R.G.A.

In Reserve.
1st Inf. Bde.
1st Bn. Machine Gun Corps (less "B" & "C" Coys & 8 guns "D" Coy.).
23rd Field Coy. R.E. (less 1 Section).
26th Field Coy. R.E. (less 1 Section).
409th Field Coy. R.E.
1/6th Bn. The Welch Regt. (Pioneers).

Attached. To Div. H.Q. from IX Corps Cyclist Bn. -
1 Officer and 24 Other Ranks.

/ (b)...............

SECRET

NARRATIVE OF OPERATIONS OF 1st DIVISION ON 24th SEPTEMBER, 1918.

(a) ORDER OF BATTLE.

G.O.C. Major-General E.P. STRICKLAND, C.B., C.M.G., D.S.O.

2nd Inf. Bde.
Brigadier-General G.C. KELLY.

2nd Bn. The Royal Sussex Regt.
1st Bn. The Northamptonshire Regt.
2nd Bn. The King's Royal Rifle Corps.
2nd Trench Mortar Battery.

Attached.
"B" Coy. 1st Bn. Machine Gun Corps.
1 Section 23rd Field Coy. R.E.
Nos. 4 and 5 Sections "C" Coy. 13th Bn. Tank Corps.

3rd Inf. Bde.
Brigadier-General Sir W.A.I.KAY, Bt., C.M.G., D.S.O.

1st Bn. The South Wales Borderers.
1st Bn. The Gloucestershire Regt.
2nd Bn. The Welch Regt.
3rd Trench Mortar Battery.

Attached.
"C" Coy. 1st Bn. Machine Gun Corps.
2 Sections "D" Coy. 1st Bn. Machine Gun Corps.
1 Section 26th Field Coy. R.E.
No. 3. Section "C" Coy. 13th Bn. Tank Corps.

Operating on Right Bde. front for Smoke Barrage :-
No. 1. Special Coy. R.E. (Mortar).

Artillery.
C.R.A. Brigadier-General H.F.E. LEWIN, C.M.G.

25th Bde. R.F.A.) 1st Divl. Artillery.
39th Bde. R.F.A.)

Attached.
5th Army Bde. R.H.A.
16th Army Bde. R.H.A.
168th Bde. R.F.A. (32nd Divl. Artillery).
298th Army Bde. R.F.A.
14th Bde. R.G.A.

In Reserve.
1st Inf. Bde.
1st Bn. Machine Gun Corps (less "B" & "C" Coys & 8 guns "D" Coy.).
23rd Field Coy. R.E. (less 1 Section).
26th Field Coy. R.E. (less 1 Section).
409th Field Coy. R.E.
1/6th Bn. The Welch Regt. (Pioneers).

Attached. To Div. H.Q. from IX Corps Cyclist Bn. -
1 Officer and 24 Other Ranks.

/(b)..............

(2).

(b) DISPOSITIONS.

Detailed dispositions of troops at Zero are shewn on Map attached.

Headquarters.

1st Division.

    Advanced - POEUILLY. Q.29.d.1.4.

    Rear   - MERAUCOURT. V.12.b.6.7.

D.A.   - POEUILLY. Q.29.d.1.4.

  Right Group R.F.A.   - R.33.c.9.4.

  Left Group R.F.A.   - R.28.b.8.8.

D.E.   - POEUILLY. Q.29.d.1.4.

Field Coys. R.E. (less Sections 23rd and 26th Field Coys. attached to Inf. Bdes) and Pioneers in VERMAND - MAISSEMY Area.

Right Inf. Bde.   - 3rd Inf. Bde.   H.Q. R.35.b.7.7.

Left Inf. Bde.   - 2nd Inf. Bde.   H.Q. R.29.d.9.6.

13th Bn. Tank Corps. - POEUILLY. Q.29.d.1.4.

Reserve Inf. Bde. - 1st Inf. Bde.   H.Q. R.32.b.1.2.

    Troops in VERMAND - CAULAINCOURT Area.

* * *

(3).

(c). BRIEF PLAN OF THE OPERATIONS.

The object of these operations was to deny the enemy observation from the high ground S.E. of PONTRUET from which he could have seen and interfered with prospective major operations on the part of the rest of the Army to capture the HINDENBURG LINE from BELLENGLISE Northwards. The 1st Division were told to carry out this task. The plan drawn up by the Division both as regards objectives and method of attack and date were accepted by the Corps. It appeared necessary to secure the Sunken Road on the high ground 1000 yards North of GRICOURT to achieve the object of the Army. Further progress along this spur though advisable did not seem to be necessary and would entail a very awkward salient in the line which would have to be held until the major attack developed on the left. The possession of GRICOURT did not seem essential and therefore it was omitted from the objectives (this village was captured during the operations on the initiative of the Bde. on the spot). The enemy position at FRESNOY was the main obstacle. His Machine Gun nests in MARRONNIERS WOOD had to be captured or neutralized if any progress further North had to be made. The position was so strong in FRESNOY that any plan based on capturing it according to time table was very liable to fail.

The method of attack decided on therefore, was to neutralize the enemy in MARRONNIERS WOOD and CORNOUILLERS WOOD by fire while the attack passed these positions both on the right and, more important still, on the left straight up to the real objective on the high ground, FRESNOY and the WOODS in the Valley being mopped up afterwards. It was realised that if we could once get to our objective Machine Guns on the flank would not drive us back though Machine Guns on the flank might prevent us reaching the objective.

The Divl. plan entailed an advance by the 6th Div. on our right of 1200 yards. It was also necessary for the 46th Div. on our left to deal with PONTRUET.

The 6th Div. carried out an operation which so far as it concerned the immediate right of the 1st Div., was completely successful. The 46th Div. on the left decided to work down the trenches North of PONTRUET and capture the enemy's positions in that place from the rear thereby securing the left flank of the 1st Div.

The attached map shews the objectives, starting off line, Inter-Bde. and Divl. Boundaries of the 1st Div.

There were really three attacks.

On the right one Bn. of the 3rd Inf. Bde. starting in conjunction with the 6th Div. attacked from a North and South Line South of FRESNOY in a due Easterly direction extending its left as it advanced along BUGEAUD ALLEY on to its final objective ARGONNE TRENCH.

Simultaneously, with this attack 2 Bns. of the 2nd Inf. Bde. attacked from a North and South Line South of BERTHAUCOURT due East with their right on ESSLING ALLEY.

Both the above attacks to commence at Zero plus 5 minutes under a creeping barrage lifting 100 yards every 4 minutes.

The left Bn. of the 3rd Inf. Bde. on the right started from a taped line opposite FRESNOY at the same time and attacked N.E. through FRESNOY to its final objective. The creeping barrage in front of this Bn. however, only lifted 100 yards in every 5 minutes. This slower rate of barrage coupled with the fact that the Bn. started further West than the others enabled the ground East of FRESNOY to be neutralized by fire while the two attacks on the wings were pressing forward over the exposed ground on the flanks.

/ 12 Tanks co-operated.........

(4).

12 Tanks co-operated with the Div. 4 Tanks Mark V (2 male 1 female 1 composite) were to attack FRESNOY CEMETERY, MARRONNIERS WOOD and CORNOUILLERS WOOD approaching these objectives from the South of FRESNOY Village having moved up originally behind the right Bn. of the 3rd Inf. Bde.

8 Tanks Mark V (5 male, 1 female 2 composite) co-operated with the Bde. on the left, 6 Tanks co-operated with the main attack to the final objective the remaining 2 Tanks co-operating with the Support Bn. of this Inf. Bde. whose rôle it was, to mop up ARBOUSIERS WOOD and the Valley to CORNOUILLERS WOOD while the 3rd Inf. Bde. was moving up the other side of the Valley.

Aircraft.

Arrangements were made with the Army Wing to -

(a) Attack with bombs immediately East of the creeping barrage MUGUET WOOD and the Sunken Road just West of it and SAMPSON, CHEVILLARD and DAVID TRENCHES.

(b) To neutralise with Smoke the "THREE SAVAGES" (East of GRICOURT and GLOUTONS TRENCH in the neighbourhood of GALOPINS ALLEY.

(c) To neutralise with Smoke the Southern portion of - BLAENOY TRENCH and the high ground just East of it.

(d) To attack with Machine Guns the Sunken Road on the final objective of the 2nd Inf. Bde.

Machine Guns.

32 Machine Guns were used in conjunction with Artillery at the commencement of the creeping barrage. 8 of these guns moved forward as soon as the barrage work ceased to reinforce the rear guns working with Inf. Bdes. and form a strong Machine Gun Defence in depth on the ground captured by the attack. These guns were in addition to the Coy. working with each Inf. Bde.

Arrangements were made in the plan to push up a Field Coy. R.E. and a Coy. of the Pioneer Bn. on each Bde. front to consolidate and wire the final objectives when won and arrangements were also made by the O.C. M.G. Bn. to organise Batteries to neutralise enemy Machine Guns and to harass enemy Infantry by day and night.

(d). ACCOUNT OF THE ACTION.

Zero hour was at 5 a.m.

There was some shelling during the assembly of troops but few casualties and the attack started according to programme. On the right the right Bn. of the 3rd Inf. Bde. secured its objective with little loss. The simultaneous attack on the left went well and elements reached their final objective on the Sunken Road up to time but heavy casualties were inflicted on the left flank from PONTRUET where the attempt by the 46th Div. to capture PONTRUET failed with the result that PONTRUET and the trenches at the South Western end remained in the enemy's hands throughout the operations, enfilading all movement to the South and inflicting heavy losses on the 1st Bn. Northamptonshire Regt. The elements of units which reached the Sunken Road were practically annihilated by shell-fire and enfilade Machine Gun fire and the position became untenable.

/ The left Bn...............

The left Bn. had to throw a flank back to the trenches just East of BERHTAUCOURT to protect themselves from PONTRUET. On their right the 2nd Royal Sussex Regt. secured that portion of SAMPSON TRENCH on the GREEN objective and though heavily counter-attacked and very weak maintained its position all day. One Coy. of this Bn. when counter-attacked by a force of about 400 of the enemy, finding itself temporarily short of Ammunition moved out a Lewis Gun in front of the trenches and under cover of its fire delivered a bayonet charge which completely routed the counter-attack and resulted in our securing 50 prisoners.

Meanwhile on the left of the 3rd Inf. Bde. the strongly fortified position of FRESNOY CEMETERY was rapidly carried and the left Bn. of the Bde. continued to advance through MARRONNIERS WOOD but progress was slow as it was impossible to deal with the strongly fortified Machine Gun nests which remained impervious to the Artillery bombardment. Eventually the 3rd Inf. Bde. completely encircled the MARRONNIERS WOOD and got on to their BLUE objective while enemy Machine Guns were still shooting from the North-Western end of MARRONNIERS WOOD (these Machine Guns were not mopped up until after nightfall when 5 Officers and 130 men were captured here).

On the opposite side of the Valley the 2nd K.R.R.Corps (Reserve Bn. 2nd Inf. Bde) mopped up ARBOUSIERS WOOD and worked down to CORNOUILLERS WOOD. There they had to wait some time for the 3rd Inf. Bde. to work round to them and were therefore, not available as Reserve to the Bde. as early as they should have been according to plan.

This situation necessitated the Div. ordering up the 1st Cameron Highlanders from the 1st Inf. Bde. to the VILLEMAY TRENCH area as a Reserve to the 2nd Inf. Bde. in case they were wanted.

The 3rd Inf. Bde. were at the same time told that their first task was to release the 2nd K.R.R.Corps from all responsibility in the CORNOUILLERS WOOD area before attempting to go further as news had just been received that the B.G.C. was planning to capture GRICOURT.

The 3rd Inf. Bde. however, not only fulfilled its task of releasing the 2nd K.R.R.Corps but continued to arrange its plan against GRICOURT. It organised its own creeping barrage and attacked at 5.30 p.m. with complete success and very light casualties capturing ALSACE TRENCH, BEAUVRAIGNES TRENCH and BLAINOY TRENCH. As the latter was captured, the enemy delivered a counter-attack which was well organised and well executed, and as a result we temporarily lost part of BLAINOY TRENCH. The 2nd Welch Regt. however, attacked again at once, recapturing the trench and 40 prisoners. The net result of this operation was that our position was much better than if the original objective only had been consolidated and the success was due in large measures to the able appreciation of the situation made by the Brigadier on the spot.

So far the operations had been very fruitful and successful except for the fact that owing to PONTRUET still being in the enemy's hands we had failed to establish ourselves on the Sunken Road which was after all, the main object of the operation.

The 2nd Inf. Bde. however, as soon as the 2nd K.R.R.Corps became available from the CORNOUILLERS WOOD area pushed this Bn. up into SAMPSON TRENCH and then waited for dusk. The Bde. then organised a short crash bombardment on the Sunken Road which put the enemy garrison to flight and the 2nd K.R.R.Corps advanced and secured the objective without any casualties. During the night the Field Coys. and Pioneer Coys. helped the Infantry to consolidate and wired the front.

/ The 2nd Inf. Bde..........

The 2nd Inf. Bde. was now very weak after two big attacks on the 18th and 24th September. The Bde. was told however, that it was necessary to hold the ground gained without relief until the major operation on our left developed and it was also asked to release the 1st Camerons so that the latter could rest and refit in view of future operations. The general situation was explained to the tired and depleted Bns. by the Brigadier and a Divl. Staff Officer on the morning of the 25th and each Bn. Commander said they would hold their position without the support of the Cameron Highlanders. In saying this, they knew that they would be counter-attacked on the Sunken Road as actually occurred at least once on the 25th. The Bns. however, maintained every inch of the ground which they had gained and completely achieved the object set to the Div. by the Army. Meanwhile, the release of the Cameron Highlanders enabled the 1st Division to have a Bde. sufficiently fresh to carry out successfully the trying operations it was called upon to perform in co-operation with the Fourth Army attack on the HINDENBURG LINE on the 29th and 30th September.

The casualties of the Div. on the 24th were -

        Killed   - 12 Officers, 83 Other Ranks.
        Wounded - 35 Officers, 430 Other Ranks.
        Missing - 64 Other Ranks.

Captures in prisoners and material were :-

Prisoners (Unwounded - 21 Officers, 943 Other Ranks.
              (Wounded   - 3 Officers, 132 Other Ranks.

Material.   4 - 77 mm. Guns.
             4 H.T.Ms.
             9 L.T.Ms.
             2 Anti-Tank Rifles.
             Large number of Machine Guns (total not counted).

* * *

W.O 95 / 1266

ATTACK BY 1ST DIVISION.
24-9-16.

SUPERIMPOSED ON SHEET 62B.
Scale 1:40,000.

SECRET

NARRATIVE OF OPERATIONS OF 1st DIVISION
29th SEPTEMBER to 3rd OCTOBER, 1918.

This is a S E C R E T Document.

No copies are to be made.

The recipient is responsible that the instructions contained in D.R.O. No. 936 dated 21/10/18 are complied with.

* *

    1st Trench Mortar Battery.

Attached.
    "A" Coy. 1st Bn. Machine Gun Corps.
    1 Section 409th Field Coy. R.E.

3rd Inf. Bde.
    Brigadier-General Sir W.A.I. KAY, Bt., C.M.G., D.S.O.

    1st Bn. The South Wales Borderers.
    1st Bn. The Gloucestershire Regt.
    2nd Bn. The Welch Regt.
    3rd Trench Mortar Battery.

Attached.
    "C" Coy. 1st Bn. Machine Gun Corps.
    1 Section 23rd Field Coy. R.E.

Artillery.
    C.R.A.   Brigadier-General H.F.E. LEWIN, C.M.G.

    25th Bde. R.F.A. } 1st Divl. Artillery.
    39th Bde. R.F.A. }

Attached.
    5th Army Bde. R.H.A.
    298th Army Bde. R.F.A.

In Reserve.
    2nd Inf. Bde.
    1st Bn. Machine Gun Corps (less "A" & "C" Coys).
    23rd Field Coy. R.E. (less 1 Section).
    26th Field Coy. R.E.
    409th Field Coy. R.E. (less 1 Section).
    1/6th Bn. The Welch Regt. (Pioneers).

* *

SECRET

NARRATIVE OF OPERATIONS OF 1st DIVISION
29th SEPTEMBER to 3rd OCTOBER, 1918.

(a) ORDER OF BATTLE.

    G.O.C. Major-General E.P. STRICKLAND, C.B., C.M.G., D.S.O.

    1st Inf. Bde.
        Brigadier-General L.L. WHEATLEY, C.M.G., D.S.O.

        1st Bn. The Black Watch (Royal Highlanders).
        1st Bn. The Loyal North Lancashire Regt.
        1st Bn. Queen's Own Cameron Highlanders.
        1st Trench Mortar Battery.

    Attached.
        "A" Coy. 1st Bn. Machine Gun Corps.
        1 Section 409th Field Coy. R.E.

    3rd Inf. Bde.
        Brigadier-General Sir W.A.I. KAY, Bt., C.M.G., D.S.O.

        1st Bn. The South Wales Borderers.
        1st Bn. The Gloucestershire Regt.
        2nd Bn. The Welch Regt.
        3rd Trench Mortar Battery.

    Attached.
        "C" Coy. 1st Bn. Machine Gun Corps.
        1 Section 23rd Field Coy. R.E.

    Artillery.
      C.R.A. Brigadier-General H.F.E. LEWIN, C.M.G.

        25th Bde. R.F.A. } 1st Divl. Artillery.
        39th Bde. R.F.A. }

    Attached.
        5th Army Bde. R.H.A.
        298th Army Bde. R.F.A.

    In Reserve.
        2nd Inf. Bde.
        1st Bn. Machine Gun Corps (less "A" & "C" Coys).
        23rd Field Coy. R.E. (less 1 Section).
        26th Field Coy. R.E.
        409th Field Coy. R.E. (less 1 Section).
        1/6th Bn. The Welch Regt. (Pioneers).

(b). DISPOSITIONS.

    Detailed dispositions of troops at Zero are shewn on Map attached.

Headquarters.

1st Division.	Advanced.	POEUILLY.	Q.29.d.1.4.
	Rear.	MERAUCOURT.	

D.A.	POEUILLY.	Q.29.d.1.4.
Right Group R.F.A.		R.23.b.4.5.
Left Group R.F.A.		R.23.b.4.5.

D.E.   POEUILLY.   Q.29.d.1.4.

    Field Coys. R.E. (less Sections 23rd and 409th Field Coys. attached to Inf. Bdes) and Pioneers in VERMAND - MAISSEMY Area.

Right Bde.	3rd Inf. Bde.	H.Q.	R.23.b.4.4.
Left Bde.	1st Inf. Bde.	H.Q.	R.23.b.4.4.
Reserve Bde.	2nd Inf. Bde.	H.Q.	R.32.b.1.2.

* *

(3).

(c). BRIEF PLAN OF THE OPERATIONS.

The Fourth Army were to storm the main HINDENBURG Defences on the 29th September, the IX Corps again being on the right of the Army. The 46th Div. of the IX Corps had the task of capturing the HINDENBURG LINE about BELLENGLISE and to put them on their attacking front, the 1st Division side-slipped to the left on the night 26/27th September, 1st Inf. Bde. from Divl. Reserve about VERMAND relieving the right Bde. of the 46th Div. while the left Bde. of the 6th Div. on our right relieved the 3rd Inf. Bde. which came into Divl. Reserve at VERMAND. The plan of operations as they affected the 1st Div. was as follows :-

On the left of the IX Corps the 46th Div. was to carry out the main attack advancing directly on BELLENGLISE from the high ground West of it and having crossed the Canal was to make 5 bounds to an objective which took them West of LEHAUCOURT with their right on the Canal.

Behind the 46th Div. the 32nd Div. were to follow up and leap-frog the 46th Div. and carry on to a further objective which would take them East of LEVERGIES.

The right of the Corps was held by the 6th Div. who were to hold their present front keeping touch with the enemy by means of patrols in case he retired.

The 1st Div. had to detail a detachment to advance with the right of the 46th Div. and to form a defensive flank between PONTRUET and the Canal at BELLENGLISE while the 46th Div. crossed the Canal. It had also to keep the enemy engaged on the high ground South of the Canal and East of PONTRUET.

Its further task was to secure the THORIGNY and TALANA HILL Ridge as soon as the 32nd Div. passed through the 46th Div. East of LEHAUCOURT on the other side of the Canal and then to push on and join hands with the 32nd Div. on the Canal S.E. of LE TRONQUOY.

In detail the 1st Div. plan to carry out above is shewn in the following extracts from Divl. Instructions :-

Direct co-operation with 46th Div.

(a). "Under orders of C.R.A. IX Corps both Artillery Groups will put a smoke barrage down on the East and West Grid Line through M.12.central from N.8.central to M.10.central.

By Zero plus 2 hours 30 mins remaining smoke resources will not suffice for more than 1 Artillery Bde. in each Group and C.R.A. will arrange that at that hour 1 Bde. in each Group shall come under the orders of B.Gs.C. 3rd and 1st Inf. Bdes. respectively.

Unless required for co-operation with Inf. Bdes. these Artillery Bdes. will continue barrage work with H.E. as directed by C.R.A.

(b) B.G.C., 1st Inf. Bde. in consultation with O.C. M.G. Bn. will arrange for an enfilade barrage of, if possible, 8 M.Gs at Zero hour on FLUTE TRENCH in M.4.b. and 5.c.

(c) No.1. Special Coy. R.E. is arranging a smoke barrage in M.17.a. from Zero plus 60 mins to screen the 46th Div. from high ground in M.17. No.1. Special Coy. R.E. will keep an Officer at 3rd Inf. Bde. H.Q. who can stop the smoke discharge if and when, 3rd Inf. Bde. can seize this high ground.

(d). 1st Inf. Bde.............

(4).

(d). 1st Inf. Bde. will detail a detachment to advance under the right of 46th Div. creeping barrage at Zero to secure the bank and dug-outs in G.34.c.central. and to form a defensive flank while 46th Div. crosses the Canal. This detachment will be accompanied by M.Gs to fire in enfilade on the enemy trenches in M.4.b.

Indirect co-operation with 46th Div.

(a). 3rd Inf. Bde. by active patrolling will try to ascertain enemy's dispositions on high ground in M.17. If strong enemy resistance is encountered a fire fight with Infantry and M.Gs is to be commenced - only sufficient force will be employed in the first instance, to keep the enemy fully occupied.

On receipt of information that the 46th Div. are across the Canal pressure can be gradually increased and Artillery will be available to co-operate under B.G.C. after Zero plus 2 hours 30 mins.

As soon as enemy resistance weakens or if patrols meet no resistance, FAUCILLE TRENCH in M.17.b. and 11.d. will be captured, a defensive flank being thrown back to ALSACE TRENCH.

A further advance to trenches in M.12.c. will be carried out at discretion of B.G.C. at any time, but any further advance must depend on the ability of 1st Inf. Bde. to advance Eastwards South of the Canal to approximately the Sunken Road in M.12.a. and M.5.d.

In the above operations B.G.C. 3rd Inf. Bde. will keep both the Artillery and No.1. Special Coy. R.E. posted at all times as to his intentions.

(b). 1st Inf. Bde. after forming the defensive flank mentioned in para. 6 will arrange to keep in close touch with progress of 46th Div. and as soon as BLUE objective is gained, will commence to push forward on the South bank of the Canal towards the Sunken Road in M.4.c.d. and b.

As 46th Div. progresses from BROWN to YELLOW objectives, 1st Inf. Bde. will again fight forward South of the Canal to the Sunken Road in M.12.a. and 5.d. For this operation, B.G.C. will keep the Artillery posted as to his intentions. After Zero plus 2 hours 30 mins, 1 Bde. R.F.A. will be at his disposal.

(c). After gaining the line of the Sunken Road mentioned above, further objectives will be given from Div. H.Q.: they will probably be :-

3rd Inf. Bde. - THORIGNY and TALANA HILL.
1st Inf. Bde. - TALANA HILL (exclusive) to Canal about N.8.b. central."

3rd Inf. Bde. relieved the 2nd Inf. Bde. on the right Sector of the Divl. front on the night 28/29th. The 2nd Inf. Bde. which was very weak and tired was brought into Reserve at VERMAND.

Dispositions at Zero hour on the 29th are shewn on attached map.

/ (d) Account of the Action....

(5).

(d). ACCOUNT OF THE ACTION.

29th. Zero hour was at 05.50. The operations were favoured by very thick mist practically amounting to a fog which did not clear until after 9 a.m.

The 46th Div. attack went without a hitch. The Left Bn. of the 1st Inf. Bde. (1st L.N.Lancs) had little difficulty so far as the enemy were concerned in protecting the right of the 46th Div. and cleared up all the trenches West of the Canal and North of the ST. HELENE - BELLENGLISE Road capturing 40 or 50 prisoners. The main difficulty in this task was keeping direction and cohesion in the thick mist, but the Bn. overcame this difficulty successfully. Meanwhile the Black Watch on their right pushed forward from PONTRUET and cleared the trenches just N.E. of that place. They then pushed forward their left, joined hands with the L.N.Lancs on the PONTRUET - BELLENGLISE Road and commenced to fight their way forward due East on the South bank of the Canal, the L.N.Lancs being squeezed out into support.

While the above was taking place the 3rd Inf. Bde. pushed forward portions of the 1st Gloster Regt. along the high ground a mile S.E. of PONTRUET. The enemy was found holding the trenches on this spur in strength just West of SYCOMORES WOOD. It was not in the plan to launch a strong frontal attack against these trenches and the Glosters were therefore held up on this high ground until the trenches were eventually cleared from the North. This did not happen until after dark. Throughout this operation the 3rd Inf. Bde. had to throw back a long flank to North of GRICOURT to the 6th Div. who were not supposed to advance.

On the left of the 3rd Inf. Bde. the S. Wales Borderers in touch with the Black Watch of the 1st Inf. Bde., captured successively the two lines of trenches North of the high ground on which the Glosters were held up. This Bn. swung its left up and gradually fought its way forward on to the high ground by ROOD WOOD while the Black Watch made the line of the BELLENGLISE - ST. QUENTIN Road on their left.

During the afternoon, the Black Watch at one time progressed beyond this road but were unable to make headway owing to enfilade M.G. fire from the high ground on the South.

Meanwhile North of the Canal the 32nd Div. in the afternoon leap-frogged the 46th Div. and made their objectives East of LEVERGIES and secured LE TRONQUOY.

During the night 29/30th the situation on the high ground about SYCOMORES WOOD and East of ROOD WOOD was cleared up by the South Wales Borderers who mopped up the GLU TRENCH and FORESTIER TRENCH as far as FUMIATES ALLEY inclusive.

During this night, the 6th Div. on our right was relieved by the 47th French Div.

The task of the 1st Div. for the 30th was to secure THORIGNY and TALANA HILL with left flank on the Canal South of LE TRONQUOY where touch was to be gained with 32nd Div.

The 3rd Inf. Bde. was ordered to organise an attack along the high ground ROOD WOOD to THORIGNY and to capture the latter and TALANA HILL arranging a barrage with Artillery Group. One Bde. of the Left Artillery Group was placed at disposal of B.G.C. for this purpose in addition to the right Group. 1st Inf. Bde. was ordered to fight forward on the low ground between the ridge and the Canal in co-operation.

A Bn. of Tanks had on the 29th moved up to near VERMAND and in the evening moved to near BERTHAUCOURT.

/ Arrangements........

Arrangements were made during the night for 5 of these Tanks to move up and assist the 3rd Inf. Bde. in the morning. As a matter of fact, owing to engine trouble and other technical difficulties only 1 Tank materialised with the Infantry on the 30th and this one was not really required.

The 3rd Inf. Bde. attacked and captured THORIGNY and TALANA HILL on the morning of the 30th with little opposition. On their left the 1st Black Watch of the 1st Inf. Bde. fought its way forward very successfully keeping touch with the operations on the high ground capturing about 200 prisoners.

During the afternoon of the 30th and night 30th Sept/Oct.1st the 3rd Inf. Bde. relieved all the 1st Inf. Bde. South of the Canal at LE TRONQUOY and the 1st Inf. Bde. put in the 1st Cameron Highlanders and the L.N.Lancs to relieve the 32nd Div. between LE TRONQUOY and LEVERGIES.

Meanwhile, the 47th French Div. on our right had orders in the afternoon to attack from GRICOURT South of THORIGNY and TALANA HILL and as they cleared the front of the 3rd Inf. Bde. to relieve the latter on the high ground.

The French attack in the afternoon was held up at once by M.Gs from GLOUTONS TRENCH and no progress was made that night.

(Adv. Div. H.Q. moved to MAISSEMY at 16.00).

On October 1st, the French fought their way forward gradually towards the Canal South of LE TRONQUOY and in the afternoon the 3rd Inf. Bde. was relieved of all responsibility for the right flank and came into Support in the area South of the Canal between LE TRONQUOY, ROOD WOOD and the Canal Bridge at LEHAUCOURT.

During the 2nd only the 1st Inf. Bde. and the Divisional Artillery were engaged. The role of the 1st Inf. Bde. was to keep touch with the left of the 32nd Div. on the LE TRONQUOY - SEQUEHART Ridge and also with the left of the 47th French Div. who were passing over the Canal at LE TRONQUOY and attacking S.E.

The 1st L.N.Lancs were employed by the 1st Inf. Bde. to keep touch with the 32nd Div and the 1st Cameron Highlanders to ensure touch between the L.N.Lancs and the French. It was an unsatisfactory day from a Divl. point of view as on the left the 32nd Div. were driven out of SEQUEHART by counter attack and on the right the French came on to the high ground by LE TRONQUOY occupied by the Camerons but failed to make any appreciable progress all day. The net result was that our two Bns. though not actually engaged suffered considerable casualties from enemy shell-fire on the Ridge between LE TRONQUOY and SEQUEHART which became very congested with troops.

The best information as to the actual state of affairs, both on the 32nd Div. and 47th French Div. fronts emanated periodically throughout the day, from the L.N.Lancs and 1st Cameron Highlanders.

The Divl. Artillery co-operated throughout the day with the French both Groups being South of the Canal, forward Bdes. of each Group in the Valley North of THORIGNY and Rear Bdes. N.W. of SYCOMORES WOOD.

On the 3rd instant, the role of both the 1st Inf. Bde. and the Divl. Artillery remained the same. The 32nd Div. on the left had orders this day to capture SEQUEHART and advance N.E. beyond it. The 47th French Div. were to attack on a 1,500 yards front S.E. from the LE TRONQUOY high ground with their right on the Canal.

/ These attacks..........

These attacks were not only divergent, but there was 5 hours interval between their Zero hours. This complicated the task of the 1st Inf. Bde. who had to keep touch with both.

The 32nd Div. actually attacked SEQUEHART from the North with the result that to obtain touch the 1st L.N.Lancs had to extend nearly 1,500 yards beyond the Divl. Boundary laid down and had to occupy the South-Eastern half of SEQUEHART village itself. This was done on the initiative on the Bn. which thereby got absorbed in the fighting and repulsed an enemy counter-attack against the Southern portion of SEQUEHART, using the bayonet and capturing 30 or 40 prisoners. Had the French made progress the 1st Cameron Highlanders were ready to fill any gap that might occur, but as a matter of fact, the French made practically no progress throughout the day. The situation reports from the Cameron Highlanders as to the general situation were again very valuable.

About midday the 32nd Div. relieved the portion of the L.N.Lancs in SEQUEHART.

Meanwhile, the 3rd Inf. Bde. though close up to the fighting was resting and re-fitting with a view to being fresh for further operations.

At 18.30 this Bde. was placed at the disposal of the 46th Div., who, on the left of the 32nd Div. had had a successful and heavy day's fighting at the end of which, the situation on their front was rather obscure on a line which formed a salient North of the 32nd Div. 3rd Inf. Bde. moved off in the dark to take up an un-reconnoitred position in the German trenches known as the BEAUREVOIR - FONSOMME LINE East of JONCOURT.

Just at dusk, the French 47th Div. stated that orders had been received from Marshal FOCH for the French to relieve the British troops as far North as CHARDON VERT just S.W. of SEQUEHART. This would entail the relief of the 1st Inf. Bde.

No British orders to this effect were received by the Div. but shortly afterwards the 1st Inf. Bde. reported that the French troops to carry out the relief had arrived and during the night the relief was successfully accomplished. The 1st Black Watch who were in process of relieving the L.N.Lancs when the French arrived, succeeded not only in taking over the new front themselves but in handing it over again to the French during the night.

In view of the move of the 3rd Inf. Bde. the 2nd Inf. Bde. was ordered to move on the 4th from VERMAND where it had been resting since the 29th September inclusive, to the area vacated by the 3rd Inf. Bde.

The situation on the morning of the 4th was therefore :-

3rd Inf. Bde. under the 46th Div. East of JONCOURT.
1st Inf. Bde. after a relief which took all night, assembling South of the Canal between LEHAUCOURT and LE TRONQUOY.
2nd Inf. Bde. marching from VERMAND to the area South of the Canal S.W. of LEHAUCOURT.

At 10.00 at a Divl. Commanders' Conference by the Corps Commander, the Div. was ordered to move to the VRAIGNES Area into Reserve, the 3rd Inf. Bde. to remain in Reserve to the 46th Div. until the night 5/6th.

2nd Inf. Bde. was at once ordered back to CAULAINCOURT Area.

1st Inf. Bde. was ordered to march in the afternoon to VERMAND Area (1st L.N.Lancs owing to lateness of relief were left behind near LE TRONQUOY and actually rejoined the Bde. on the 5th).

/ The Divl. Arty........

The Divl. Artillery remained co-operating with the French.

The above moves were carried out as ordered during the 4th with the exception of the 1st L.N.Lancs.

Meanwhile, the 46th Div. obtained Corps approval to put the 3rd Inf. Bde. into the line on the night 4/5th while they adjusted and re-organised their Bdes.

During the day the Div. had the great misfortune to lose Brigadier-General Sir W.A.I. KAY, Commanding, 3rd Inf. Bde. and his Brigade-Major Capt. SOMERVAIL who were both killed by an enemy shell East of JONCOURT.

On the 5th, the Divl. H.Q. moved to VRAIGNES and on the night 5/6th the 3rd Inf. Bde. were relieved on the 46th Div. front and moved to their old area South of the Canal, South of LEHAUCOURT, where, however, they did not come under the Div. but remained in Reserve to the 46th Div. for operations which were planned to take place on the 7th instant. (N.B. These operations in which the 46th Div. took part were eventually postponed to the 8th and 3rd Inf. Bde. though left in the same position was placed in Corps Reserve and not under the 46th Div. It was not actually used in the operations).

The total casualties of the Div. between September 29th and October 4th inclusive were :-

    Killed   -   5 Officers, 36 O.R.

    Wounded   -   9 Officers. 238 O.R.

    Missing   -   44 O.R.

During this period prisoners and material captured were as follows :-

    11 Officers, 930 Other Ranks.

    Material.

        Field Guns..........9
        H.V. gun............1
        Machine Guns......212
        Trench Mortars......7
        Anti-Tank Guns.....15

* *

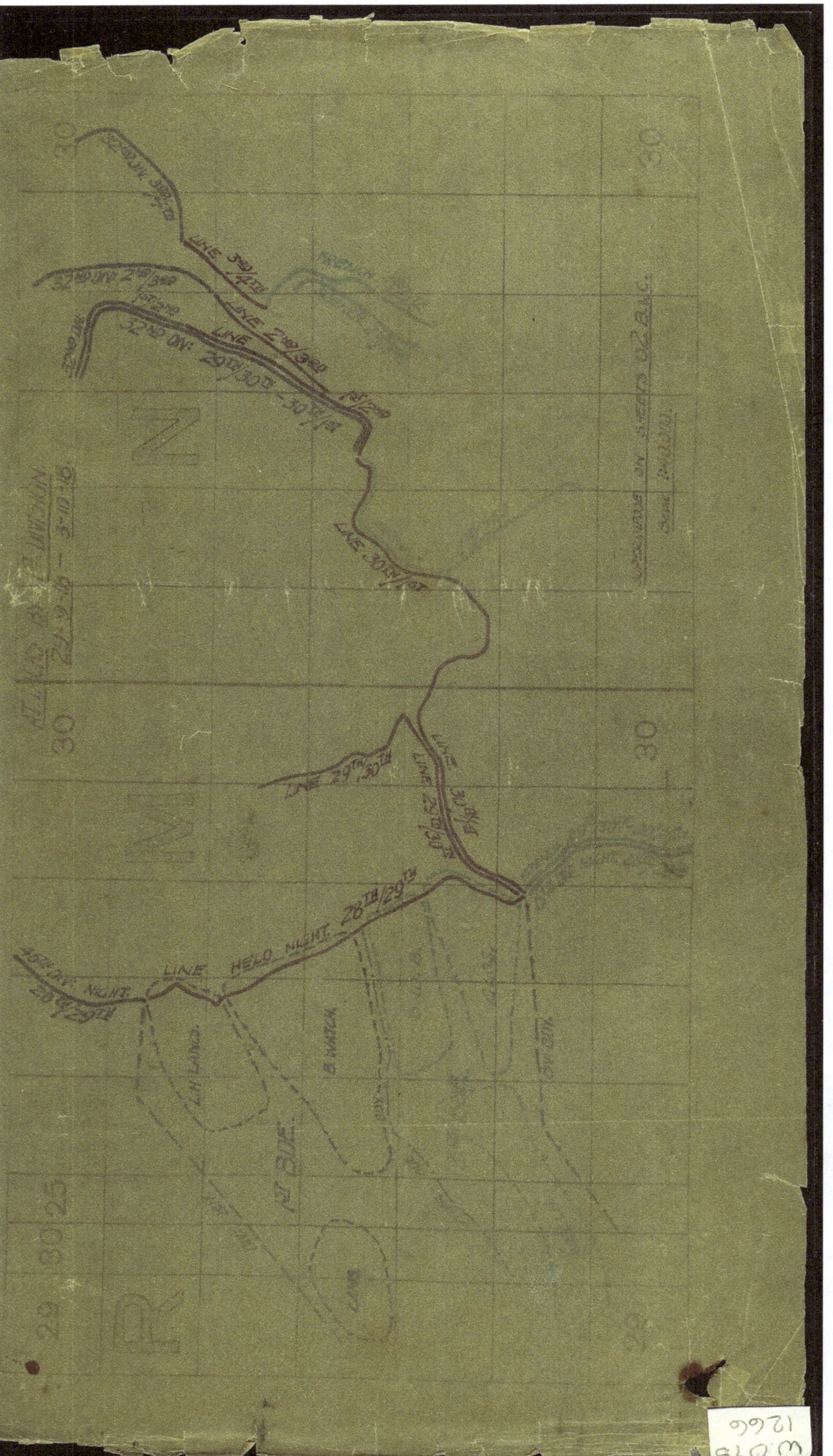

Officer Commanding,
    1st Loyal North Lancs. Regt.

    Will you please express to all ranks my appreciation of their fine work during the recent operations, and satisfaction on their excellent turn out this morning after hard and strenuous fighting.

Brigadier General,
Commanding 1st Infantry Brigade.

7th October 1918.

REPORT ON OPERATIONS 26th SEPTEMBER TO 4th OCTOBER 1918

REFERENCE MAP THORIGNY Edition 1 a.

On the night 26/27th. The Battalion took over a line about G.33.b.24 right about M.3.b.22 with advanced posts and blocks in the trenches in G.33.d.

C. Company   Left Front Company
D. Company   Right Front Company.
B. Company   Support Company.
A. Company   Reserve Company.

NIGHT 28/29th. B. Company took over a portion of the left front Company, from left to G.33.d.9.5. A. Company moved up onto PEN TRENCH in G.33.d. Advanced Battalion Headquarters established at G.33.c.
In conjunction with operations carried out by the 46th Division the Battalion formed a defensive flank.

At ZERO 5.50, Left front company, B. Company, advanced in touch with the 46th Division and established posts on the bank in B.34 Central and at B.34.d.50 supported by attached sections of M.G's. Centre Company, C. Company, established posts in the sunken road in M.4.a. x xxx xxxxxxxx xxxxxx xxxxxxxxxxx along road in M.4.a., and one at G.34.c.4.2.

A. Company keeping in close touch with the advance of the 46th Division, established posts in the sunken road in M.4.c.. Two Platoons moving under cover of bank in G.34.c. and thence along canal Bank; - two platoons moving down trenches in M.4.a.
D. Company established post in trench at M.4.c.6.5.

At ZERO plus 5½ hours the Battalion concentrated in areas M.3.b: M.4.a.: G.33.d. and G.34.c., moving at 4.30 pm into Brigade Reserve in area in M.10.c.

These operations were carried out without a hitch.

September 30th. Took over left Battalion front of Brigade Sector, relieving Dorset Regiment. Battalion Boundaries M.4.c.9.6. - H.34.d.2.7.
3 Company Front Companies distributed in depth.
Left Company   C. Company
Centre Company D. Company
Right Company   A. Company.
Support Company B. Company in ECUME TRENCH in M.5.a.

OCTOBER 1st.   Held Line.

OCTOBER 2nd.   Corps Advance continued. Battalion task to prevent gap between left Division and French Right.
Companies advanced in Artillery Formation at ZERO (8.30am) in the following order:- "C","D","A", and "B" Companies. Leading Company immediately gaining touch with Right Battalion of Right Division (Royal Scots) at H.35.a.8.3. who occupied the village of SEQUEHART. Touch with French on the right was not obtained as they were not in position reported i.e. in FLUME COPSE and FLAT IRON Wood and they did not advance.
General advance did not continue beyond this point.
The Battalion took up a line running from H.35.a.6.3. to N.4.a.7.2..
C. Company, Left front company, in touch with right brigade of 32nd Division, B. Company, Right Front Company, in touch with French Division.

B.Company,Support Company, in area C.34.d and N.4.b.
A.Company,Reserve Company, in C.34.c. and N.4.a.

OCTOBER 3rd. Previous operations were continued at ZERO 6.35 am.
C.Company pushed forward Four patrols to keep in touch with the right of left Brigade. Patrols were supported by Platoons in Artillery formation followed by "D", "A", and "B" Companies, platoons in artillery formation at a depth of 400yards per Company. Touch was maintained with left Brigade which brought the patrols to H.35.b.9.4. At this point, the Dorset Regiment moved Northward but touch was still maintained. About 7.45 am the enemy about 250 strong accompanied by light machine guns, debouched from CARISE Wood and advanced in a N.W.direction, under cover of heavy machine gun fire and attempted to work round the village of SEQUEHART from the South.
The troops in SEQUEHART were forced to withdraw. "C" "D" and "A" Coys formed a defensive flank along high ground in H.35.b. and met the enemy whom they repulsed, at the pint of the bayonet. "B" Company,Reserve Company, being in position on the high ground H.35.c. dealt with a small force of the enemy who had worked their way up on to the high ground near the bank in H.35.c. and b.

The General advance not being continued the Companies re-organised and took up their old positions as held before ZERO, gaining touch on left and right. The Battalion was relieved during the night by the 1st Black Watch and moved to the tunnel in FLECHE WOOD.

Casualties.
    Officers.
    Killed 1.
    Wounded 8
    Missing and wounded. 1.

    Other Ranks.
    Killed 27
    Wounded 212
    Missing 17

Prisoners   3 Officers 320 O.R. (Estimated)
Machine Guns. 35.

The Battalion carried out the task allotted to them i.e., to prevent there being a gap between the 32nd Division and the French, but suffered heavy casualties owing to the high ground which they were forced to hold, being heavily shelled, a large proportion of 8 inch shells being used, and swept by heavy machine gun fire from the front and right flank.

Lt-Colonel
Comdg 1st Loyal North Lancashire Regt.

REPORT ON OPERATIONS 26th SEPTEMBER TO 4th OCTOBER 1918

REFERENCE MAP TROISGNE Edition 1 a.

On the night 26/27th. The Battalion took over a line about G.33.b.24 right about M.3.b.22 with advanced posts and blocks in the trenches in G.33.d.

C. Company — Left Front Company
D. Company — Right Front Company.
B. Company — Support Company.
A. Company — Reserve Company.

NIGHT 28/29th. B.Company took over a portion of the left front Company, from left to G.33.a.9.6. A.Company moved up onto FAN TRENCH in G.33.d.
Advanced Battalion Headquarters established at G.33.c.
In conjunction with operations carried out by the 46th Division the Battalion formed a defensive flank.

At ZERO 5.50, Left front company, B.Company, advanced in touch with the 46th Division and established posts on the bank in B.34 Central and at B.34.d.50 supported by attached sections of M.G's. Centre Company, C.Company, established posts in the sunken road in M.4.a. and the xxxxxxx xxxxx xxxxxxxxxx along road in M.4.a., and one at G.34.c.4.2.

A.Company keeping in close touch with the advance of the 46th Division, established posts in the sunken road in M.4.c.. Two Platoons moving under cover of bank in G.34.c. and thence along canal Bank; — two platoons moving down trenches in M.4.a.
D.Company established post in trench at M.4.c.6.5.

At ZERO plus 5½ hours the Battalion concentrated in areas M.3.b: M.4.a.: G.33.d. and 34.c., moving at 4.30 pm into Brigade Reserve in area in M.10.c.

These operations were carried out without a hitch.

September 30th. Took over left Battalion front of Brigade Sector, relieving Dorset Regiment. Battalion Boundaries N.4.c.8.6. — H.34.d.8.7.
3 Company Front Companies distributed in depth.
Left Company — C.Company
Centre Company — D.Company
Right Company — A.Company.
Support Company — B.Company in ECOUSE TRENCH in N.5.a.

OCTOBER 1st. Held Line.

OCTOBER 2nd. Corps Advance continued. Battalion task to prevent gap between left Division and French Right.
Companies advanced in Artillery Formation at ZERO (8.30am) in the following order:— "C", "D", "A", and "B" Companies. Leading Company immediately gaining touch with Right Battalion of Right Division (Royal Scots) at H.35.a.8.3. who occupied the village of SEQUEHART. Touch with French on the right was not obtained as they were not in position reported i.e. in PLUME COPSE and FLAT IRON Wood and they did not advance.
General advance did not continue beyond this point.
The Battalion took up a line running from H.35.a.6.3. to N.4.a.7.2..
C.Company, Left Front company, in touch with right brigade of 32nd Division,
B.Company, Right Front Company, in touch with French Division.

B. Company, Support Company, in area G.34.d and N.4.b.
A. Company, Reserve Company, in G.34.c and N.4.a.

OCTOBER 3rd. Previous operations were continued at ZERO 6.55 am.
C. Company pushed forward four patrols to keep in touch with the right of left Brigade. Patrols were supported by platoons in Artillery formation followed by "D", "A", and "B" Companies, platoons in artillery formation at a depth of 400 yards per Company. Touch was maintained with left Brigade which brought the patrols to H.35.b.9.4. At this point, the Dorset Regiment moved Northward but touch was still maintained. About 7.45 am the enemy about 250 strong accompanied by light machine guns, debouched from CARISE Wood and advanced in a N.W. direction, under cover of heavy machine gun fire and attempted to work round the village of SEQUEHART from the South. The troops in SEQUEHART were forced to withdraw. "C" "D" and "A" Coys formed a defensive flank along high ground in H.35.b. and met the enemy whom they repulsed, at the point of the bayonet. "B" Company, Reserve Company, being in position on the high ground H.35.c. dealt with a small force of the enemy who had worked their way up on to the high ground near the bank in H.35.c. and b.

The General advance not being continued the Companies re-organised and took up their old positions as held before ZERO, gaining touch on left and right. The Battalion was relieved during the night by the 1st Black Watch and moved to the tunnel in FLECHE WOOD.

Casualties.
    Officers.
    Killed   1.
    Wounded   9
    Missing and wounded. 1.

    Other Ranks.
    Killed   27
    Wounded 212
    Missing 17

Prisoners   3 Officers 500 O.R. (Estimated)
Machine Guns. 35.

The Battalion carried out the task allotted to them i.e., to prevent there being a gap between the 32nd Division and the French, but suffered heavy casualties owing to the high ground which they were forced to hold, being heavily shelled, a large proportion of 8 inch shells being used, and swept by heavy machine gun fire from the front and right flank.

Lt-Colonel
Comdg 1st Loyal North Lancashire Regt.

OPERATIONS.

REPORT ON PART TAKEN BY THE 1st BATTALION LOYAL NORTH LANCASHIRE REGIMENT.

17th OCTOBER 1918.

Reference ANDIGNY FOREST 1/20000.

At 0520 hours the Battalion moved forward in a very thick mist on the right of the Camerons. Two Companies and Headquarters taking 100 degrees as their compass bearing, struck the VAUX ANDIGNY - LES FERMES Road at BELLE VUE. The arrival at BELLE VUE was at the time of the clearing of the mist and was simultaneous with the arrival of the Cameron Highlanders at this point.
Enemy were in a strong position North of BELLE VUE and the Camerons on the left suffered heavily. On arrival at the top of the ridge at the shrine of BELLE VUE the two Companies and Headquarters moved round the flanks of a large party of Germans who were under the fire of the Camerons and seing themselves out flanked, surrendered. (Number approximately 130).
Our casualties here, were 2 Killed and 1 Officer and 15 Other ranks wounded.
These two companies were then reformed and moved on LES GOBELETS which was found to be unoccupied. ANDIGNY LES FERMES was evidently occupied by the enemy, as fire was coming from that direction, so it was taken as the next objective and found to be strongly held. On realizing they were being outflanked from the NORTH EAST they surrendered and a party of about 70 prisoners in all were sent back.
Casualties in ANDIGNY LES FERMES :- 5 Killed and 5 Wounded.
These Companies were relieved during the afternoon by Companies from another Division and one was withdrawn to Battalion Headquarters at LES GOBELETS, the other moving into the Sunken Road NORTH EAST of ANDIGNY LES FERMES.
The two Companies which had lost touch will now be dealt with.
D. Company advanced approximately in the correct direction and struck the VAUX ANDIGNY - ANDIGNY LES FERMES Road between LES GOBELETS and ANDIGNY LES FERMES NORTH of the Mill and advanced to the Sunken Road running NORTH EAST E.4.D. and B. About 100 prisoners were captured near the mill.
A. Company. after crossing the REGNICOURT Road moved in the direction of the orchard West of ANDIGNY - LES FERMES. At about 0830 hours then the mist suddenly cleared, the enemy opened heavy fire with two field guns and two machine guns from the orchard. An order was given to make a man by man advance to some dead ground on the enemy's flank, the guns being kept under fire. On seeing that they were being outflanked the enemy abandoned the guns.
Casualties from these guns which were firing at point blank range :-
4 Killed and 4 wounded.
This Company then marched NORTH of the ANDIGNY LES FERMES and occupied a sunken road already occupied by D. Company.
The Battalion then had three Companies trying to work forward towards the BLANC FOSSES road and one in reserve at LES GOBELETS.
On trying to work forward on BLANC FOSSES these Companies came under very heavy machine gun fire and about 1645 hours enemy opened a heavy H.E. and Gas barrage and these Companies suffered several casualties from this barrage.
The F.O.O. was informed that machine guns had been located in the wood at FORESTERS HOUSE and a battery of field guns at E.6.d.5.8..
These three Companies were ordered to dig in for the night and remained in position during the night 17/18th.

APPROXIMATE CASUALTIES.	Officers	Other Ranks
Killed	-	16
Wounded	5	90
Missing	-	16

The majority of those marked Missing were probably killed and wounded in the very thick mist in the early stages of the attack. A search is now being made for dead bodies.

R.Berkeley

Lieut. Col.
o/c 1st Bn. Loyal N. Lancashire R.

Army Form C. 2118.

WAR DIARY
or
INTELLIGENCE SUMMARY.

(Erase heading not required.)

November 1918

Place	Date	Hour	Summary of Events and Information	Remarks and references to Appendices
			Maps. 1/40000 62 & 62A. Catechised Maps. OISE CANAL 1/40,000. NAMUR 1/100,000. SAMBRE-OISE CANAL 1/40,000.	
Wassigny	November 1st & 2nd		Platoon & Company training continued. Special training in preparation for the crossing of the SAMBRE - OISE Canal was also carried out.	HDS
-do-	3rd		During the day all preparations for the battle were completed. Special equipment i.e. life belts - folding oars - hull hooks - life lines were issued. Bn paraded at 19.20 hours, moved to assembly positions just N of the canal via REDET de BEAULIEU. This road running parallel to & about 1000x from the canal. During the march a short distance from the Farm of RIBEAUCOURT the Bn came under shell fire & our casualties were sustained - 1 man killed, 1 SM 1296 1 Cpl & 2 were wounded. On arrival at the point where the Bn was to leave the road to move into assembly position the traffic was very congested. Companies however were led into their positions in order D Coy (who also took over the outposts held by the 15 Glost Regt) A Coy, C coy, B Coy, without confusion. They were then formed up in column ready for the night. Hot soup came up in containers & men also were issued during the night. Except for a little intermittent shelling	

WAR DIARY
or
INTELLIGENCE SUMMARY.
(Erase heading not required.)

Army Form C. 2118.

Place	Date	Hour	Summary of Events and Information	Remarks and references to Appendices
			which caused no casualties, the right passed without incident. At daybreak there was a very heavy mist. Zero hour was timed for 0545 hours not about 3 minutes before that hour the machine gun barrage came down prematurely. The posts had been withdrawn 250x from the canal when the artillery barrage opened on the canal. Whilst the barrage was on the canal the bridging parties the the platoons detailed as a covering party to hold the West (our bank) of the canal doubled forward & commenced to carry out their duties the movement the barrage lifted from the canal The bridges were put in position by the R.E. bridging party assisted by one platoon of D Coy, in about 5 minutes. The first party to cross was a lewis gun section to cover the crossing. They came under short range machine gun fire, but succeeded in silencing the enemy guns capturing the teams. The companies, who had left themselves informed of the progress of the crossing now began to double forward. They crossed the canal by 2 bridges in order	

A,B,C. – Dcoy remained behind & assisted in launching ware bridges. They then waved across to the position assigned to them. The actual crossing of the Bn occupied 15 minutes after the crossing was completed by 20 minutes after ZERO. The barrage advanced parallel to the canal & halted for 40 minutes on a line about 500ˣ East of the canal. During this time there were therefore not much room for movement. The dn position of companies was A & B Coy in front. A Coy was to move N. parallel to the canal B Coy in touch with A Coy moved approximately NE. C Coy moved approximately East. D Coy was detailed as reserve Coy. During the first hour there was to the barrage lifting, a large number of the enemy were encountered – in most cases with machine guns. These were all successfully disposed of. The enemy when seeing themselves in danger of being outflanked showed themselves disposed to surrender, only in a few cases put up a strong resistance. On the lifting of the barrage, companies moved forward to their various objectives

WAR DIARY or INTELLIGENCE SUMMARY

Owing to the thickness of the mist, the operation developed into a series of hand to hand combats between small parties. Although 50% of the men of the Bn had never been in action before, the experience made a fine example of the way the experienced Officers, NCO's men of the Bn enabled them to deal with slight loss with these numerous parties. In several cases parties of 15 to 20 were surrounded in houses. The first few ex-ponts [?] were exterminated, were disposed of with bomb & bayonet, the remainder surrendered. Dealing with these posts in this way, at the same time pressing on keeping a portion of men to command up with the barrage Coy, any Officers reserved towards their Objective. Owing to the thick mist it was not possible to gain a way accurate table, but Cdn however reported their coys on the objective at the following hours - Coy 09.30 B coy 09.40 - by which time A coy had moved up to the CATILLON RD there in touch with the 3rd Bde. Day in course was consolidating East of the Canal.

WAR DIARY or INTELLIGENCE SUMMARY

Army Form C. 2118.

This completed the work so far as the occupation of the "Blue dotted line" was concerned. The brigade halted for 30 minutes in front of the Blue dotted line, when it & "A" & "B" Coys moved forward to take up its final objective. By this time the mist had cleared & B Coy occupied their final objective with only slight opposition. 1st The Black Watch moved through the Bn to their objective & except on the CATILLON Rd (ROUTE NATIONALE No 29) the Bn was squeezed out on this account. C Coy, which was fulfilling mobile, received orders to concentrate in M.27.c. Orders were received at 1900 hrs L.E. Coy moved up in case they were required by O.C. 1st Cameron Hrs. Placed under the orders of that Officer. So far as the Bn was concerned, no further development took place + at about 1700 hrs orders were received that the Bde would be relieved by a Bde of the 46th Division. At 2300 hrs the last carrying relieved, the Bn concentrated in MOLAIN. Total casualties - 7 ORs killed, 41 ORs wounded, 4 ORs missing.

Army Form C. 2118.

WAR DIARY
or
INTELLIGENCE SUMMARY.
(Erase heading not required.)

Instructions regarding War Diaries and Intelligence Summaries are contained in F. S. Regs., Part II. and the Staff Manual respectively. Title pages will be prepared in manuscript.

Place	Date	Hour	Summary of Events and Information	Remarks and references to Appendices
	November			
			Prisoners captured - approximately 400.	
			Material captured - 5 field guns & trench mortars 36 Heavy & 46 light Machine Guns.	
			The operations were very successful, the division as a whole was highly complimented by both the Army & Corps Commanders	WD
RIBEAUVILLE	5th		Bn marched to Villers en MOLAIN	WD
MOLAIN	6th		Bn marched to Camp in FRESNOY le GRAND. missing in very heavy rain at Botha	WD
FRESNOY le GRAND	7th		Day devoted to reorganisation, cleaning up etc.	WD
	8th-12th		These days were spent in company and platoon training, special attention being paid to drill and equipment.	Rosie
	11th		The armistice signed came into force at 11:00 hours.	Rosie
GRAND FAYT	13th		The Battalion marched by busses to GRAND FAYT, a village on the lesser ELBE, near CARTIGNIES.	Rosie
	14th		This day was devoted to kit inspections and internal economy.	Rosie
SARS POTERIES	15th		The Battalion marched to SARS POTERIES near SOLRE LE CHATEAU	Rosie

Army Form C. 2118.

WAR DIARY
or
INTELLIGENCE SUMMARY.
(Erase heading not required.)

Instructions regarding War Diaries and Intelligence Summaries are contained in F. S. Regs., Part II. and the Staff Manual respectively. Title pages will be prepared in manuscript.

Place	Date	Hour	Summary of Events and Information	Remarks and references to Appendices
HESTRUD	16		The battalion marched to WILLIES in HESTRUD ready to take part in the march to the RHINE.	Route.
—	17		Day devoted to platoon training and internal economy.	
BOUSSU			The battalion marched to BOUSSU as part of its advance guard to the 1st Brigade Group, and billeted there for the night, with pickets on the eastern entrance.	Route.
LEZ-WALCOURT	18			Route.
FRAIRE	19		March continued to FRAIRE where the battalion billeted and picketed its eastern road entrances.	Route.
"	20-22		Short halt was called owing to the difficulty of bringing up supplies pending the improvement of road and railways. The time was spent in cleaning and smartening up the men both in regards personal appearance and general turn out.	
			Advance was resumed. Battalion, again marching as advance guard to Bde Group, moved to billets in FLAVION. On arrival at FLAVION Intey protection was taken over by 1st Bn The BLACK WATCH, who passed on ahead. Just before entering (Bathurst returning)	Route.
FLAVION	24			

Army Form C. 2118.

WAR DIARY
or
INTELLIGENCE SUMMARY.
(Erase heading not required.)

Instructions regarding War Diaries and Intelligence Summaries are contained in F. S. Regs., Part II. and the Staff Manual respectively. Title pages will be prepared in manuscript.

Place	Date	Hour	Summary of Events and Information	Remarks and references to Appendices
			the village, the Battalion was met by a deputation of the inhabitants who, after hearty cheers, gave an address of welcome, conducted the Bn. to its billets	
FLAVION FERME	24th		March was resumed. First destination of the Battalion was ONHAYE but on arrival billets were found to be bad, that a further move to some farms some 2 miles further East was decided on. After a 2 - 3 hour halt for dinners, the march was resumed and Battalion reached its final billets about 1600 hours. Weather throughout for the last 2 days was ideal for marching though until the sun showed the roads the heat made the going rather difficult for the horses.	
CHATEAU MEUN, ONHAYE	25"		Training for the day consisted of ceremonial parade under company arrangements. The Military Cross was awarded to Captain G. W. AINSWORTH and 2Lt (actg Captain) C. S. MacLean, both for gallantry in action at ESNES and subsequent fighting. SEAGEHART, Pte ENGLISE and subsequent fighting Sergeants Wheeler in D.R.O. of 24/11/18. Afternoon devoted to football and post inspections. Parade.	

A(7883) Wt W89pM1672 50,000 4/17 Sch 59a Forms/C/2118/4

Army Form C. 2118.

WAR DIARY
or
INTELLIGENCE SUMMARY.
(Erase heading not required.)

Place	Date	Hour	Summary of Events and Information	Remarks and references to Appendices
CHATEAU MELIN ONHAYE	26th		A battalion parade was ordered but cancelled owing to rain and the day spent on cleaning parades, kit inspections and lectures.	
			Out-standing Lewis Gun actions were (unfavourably) distributed on this date.	Ref E
	27th		The following decorations were announced to gallantry in the crossing of the SAMBRE-OISE CANAL near CATILLON: 23928 A/Sgt J. LIVESEY A Coy	A Coy
			D.C.M. Military Medal to Military Medal 19341 Sgt E. SMITH 23736 Pte A CLAYTON 26926 Pte G HOFFMAN all HQ Coy, 16475 Pte J PARKER 23589	
			Cpl A POTTER 16119 Pte T SNAPE 12233 Pte A DASBURY all B Coy, 27833 Pte	
			G MILLS 21252 L/Cpl W BENTHAM 29356 Sjt J.F HARVEY 25404 L/Cpl W	
			SHARRATT 28829 Pte R NORRIS all of C Coy, Bar and 12538 L/Cpl J SPELLMAN 22035	
			Sjt R DAVIES DCM RDCM	
			Inspection in the dot Counselled of parades by companies afternoon	Ref E
			recreational training	
	28th		Battalion paraded for route march - WEILLEN - ONHAYE - CHATEAU MELIN	
			A Coy moved billets in the afternoon from LA FERME HENLEM to FERME WESEN	
			a mile E of first introduction DEBNANT owing to an outbreak of Spanish	

Army Form C. 2118.

WAR DIARY
or
INTELLIGENCE SUMMARY.
(Erase heading not required.)

Place	Date	Hour	Summary of Events and Information	Remarks and references to Appendices
CHATEAU NEUF	28 (cont)		Tour in their previous billet.	RASE.
	29th		Battalion ceremonial parade carried out by B Coy billet. In the afternoon 'A' Coy beat 'C' Coy at football (3-1) in the CHATEAU Grounds.	RASE.
	30th		Brigade usual Infantry movements. In cleaning and preparation for transfer to RUYSSE-KENVERRED on 1st.xii.18. Contain paid out. The owner of the GROTTO CAVES DURANT threw open the [?] change to the battalion in the afternoon. By the 30th Billetting under battalion arrangements took place during the day at Brigade headquarters INTUYEN. Fighting Strength of the Battalion on 30th November was 36 Officers and 856 ORs.	RASE.

R.R. Beckley. Lieut. Col.
Commdg. 1st Bn, Loyal N. Lancashire Regt.

30-11-18

NARRATIVE OF OPERATIONS OF 1st DIVISION
4th November, 1918.

(a) ORDER OF BATTLE.

G.O.C. - Major-General E.P. STRICKLAND, C.B., C.M.G., D.S.O.

1st Inf. Bde. (Left Bde)

Brigadier-General L.L. WHEATLEY, C.M.G., D.S.O.

1st Bn. The Black Watch (Royal Highlanders).
1st Bn. Loyal North Lancs. Regt.
1st Bn. Queens Own Cameron Highlanders.
1st Trench Mortar Battery.
Attached.
1 Troop Royal Scots Greys.
23rd Field Coy. R.E.
"A" Section No. 1 Special Coy R.E.
"A" Coy 1st Bn. M.G.C.

2nd Inf. Bde. (Right Bde)

Brigadier-General G.C. KELLY, D.S.O.

2nd Bn. Rl. Sussex Regt.
1st Bn. Northampton Regt.
2nd Bn. Kings Royal Rifle Corps.
2nd Trench Mortar Battery.
Attached.
1 Troop Royal Scots Greys.
409th Field Coy R.E.
"B" Section No. 1 Special Coy R.E.
"C" Coy 1st Bn. M.G.C.

3rd Inf. Bde.

Brigadier-General E.G. ST. AUBYN, D.S.O.

1st Bn. South Wales Borderers.
1st Bn. Gloucester Regt.
2nd Bn. Welch Regt.
3rd Trench Mortar Battery.
Attached.
1 Section 26th Field Coy R.E.
"D" Coy 1st Bn. M.G.C.
1 Section "A" Coy 10th Bn. Tank Corps.
298th Army Bde R.F.A. (for barrage on CATILLON).
1 Mounted Section, Div. Mounted Detachment.

ARTILLERY.

C.R.A. - Brigadier-General H.F.E. LEWIN, C.M.G.

1st Div. Artillery.
Attached.
46th Div. Artillery.
3rd Australian Div. Artillery.
5th Army Bde R.H.A.
23rd Army Bde R.F.A.
298th Army Bde R.F.A. (after CATILLON barrage).

/DIVISIONAL RESERVE.

DIVISIONAL RESERVE.

    1st Bn. M.G.C. (less "A", "C" & "D" Coys).   ) Under O.C.
    46th Bn. M.G.C. (less 1 Coy).   ) 1st Bn.
    No. 3 (R.H.G.)Bn. Guards M.G.Regt. (less 1 Coy).) M.G.C.

    26th Field Coy R.E. (less 1 Section).   )
    1/6th Welch Regt. (Pioneers).   )Under C.R.E.
    1 Section 1st Australian Tunnelling Coy R.E.)

    1 Troop Royal Scots Greys.
    3 Platoons IX Corps Cyclists.
    1 Supply Tank "D" Section No. 2 Tank Supply Coy.
    Div. Mounted Detachment (less 1 Mounted Section).

(b) DISPOSITIONS.

    Detailed dispositions of troops at Zero are shown on map attached.

    Headquarters.

1st Division.	Advanced	BELLEVUE X.13.a.
	Rear	VAUX ANDIGNY.
Div. Artillery.		BELLEVUE X.13.a.
Right Group.		Farm at X.5.a.1.2.
Left Group.		LA LOUVIERE FARM R.35.c.6.1.
CATILLON Group.		MAZINGHEIN.
Div. Engineers.		BELLEVUE X.13.a.
26th Field Coy (less 1 Section)		in MAZINGHEIN - BEAULIEU Area.
1/6th Welch (Pioneers)		LA VALLEE MULATRE.
Right Bde. (2nd).		Farm at X.5.a.1.2.
Left Bde. (1st).		LA LOUVIERE FARM R.35.c.6.1.
3rd Bde.		MAZINGHEIN.

(e) **BRIEF PLAN OF THE OPERATIONS.**

The Fourth Army in conjunction with the First French Army on its Right and the 3rd British Army on its Left resumed the attack with the object of forcing the crossing of the SAMBRE - OISE Canal, the IX Corps attacking (with the X French Corps on its Right and the XIII British Corps on its Left) on a two Division front (1st and 32nd Divisions).

1. **Preliminaries.**

The country W. of the Canal was well adapted to the concealment of troops assembling for an attack. It was enclosed with numerous high thick hedges, through which, after careful reconnaissance by day, gaps were cut by night to allow of troops moving up to their positions, which were about 300 yards from the Canal Bank, which was held by the enemy, who also had a few posts on the West Bank. The routes were taped.

The ground was low lying and fairly soft, so shallow shelters were dug to afford some protection from fire.

The digging of the trenches and the assembly of 2 complete Brigades and 2 Field Coys were carried out so successfully that the enemy were in complete ignorance of our intentions.

The weather was favourable, being dark and wet.

2. The front of the 1st Division at this time, extending from S. of PETIT CAMBRESIS (S.15.d.central) on the Right, to the Halte N.W. of CATILLON (R.23.b.4.8.) on the Left, was held by the 3rd Inf. Bde on a three battalion front, with the 1st and 2nd Inf. Bdes in Support and Reserve respectively.

For the purposes of assembling troops of the 1st and 2nd Inf. Bdes it was necessary for these two Brigades to relieve portions of the outpost line of the 3rd Inf. Bde opposite the proposed Bridge crossings over the Canal. This was done just prior to Zero, the length of front taken over and the Inter-Bde Boundary being as shewn on the attached map.

The general plan of the operations is explained by the following extracts from 1st Division Battle Instructions.

3. On a date "Z" which has been communicated to all concerned, the 1st Division will force the passage of the SAMBRE - OISE Canal between PETIT CAMBRESIS and CATILLON. Zero hour will be in the early morning. Simultaneous attacks are being delivered by :-

  68th French Div. on the Right opposite OISY.
  32nd Div. on the Left N. of ORS.

4. Attached map shews 1st Objective (BLUE DOTTED), 2nd Objective (BLUE), 3rd Objective (RED) and defensive flanks to be formed until touch with neighbouring Divisions is assured on RED Objective (RED DOTTED). Inter-Div. Boundaries, also Inter-Bde Boundaries on 1st Div. front are shewn.

5. The attacks of the three Divs. concerned will, though simultaneous, be independent as regards detailed execution and each Div. is arranging as it advances to protect its flanks.

The points where definite touch is to be established between 1st Div. and Flank Divs. at various stages of the operations are:-

<u>With 68th French Div.</u>
 (a) Inter-Div. Boundary W. of Canal until touch has been established at (b) - (3rd Inf. Bde responsible).

/(b) Cross Roads

(b) Cross Roads LA JUSTICE (S.11.d.) - (2nd Inf. Bde responsible).

With 32nd Div.
(a) M.20.b.0.8. until touch has been established at (b) - (3rd Inf. Bde responsible).

(b) N.E. of LA GROISE (M.17.c.0.0.) - (1st Inf. Bde responsible).

6. The 46th Div. is in Corps Reserve and its head will be on the line of the MAZINGHEIN - BAZUEL Road by Zero hour on "Z" day. Its role is to move by bounds as the 1st Div. progresses with a view to relieving the 1st Div. either on the RED Objective or after any immediate exploitation which may be ordered during the operation has been completed.

7. The 1st Div. attack will be carried out by the 2nd Inf. Bde on the Right and the 1st Inf. Bde on the Left. The 3rd Inf. Bde will carry out a subsidiary and simultaneous operation to capture CATILLON and form a Bridgehead there.

8. **Main Operations of Forcing the Passage of the Canal by by 1st and 2nd Inf. Bdes.**

At Zero hour under cover of a heavy crash barrage the Right and Left Inf. Bdes will force the passage of the SAMBRE - OISE Canal - the Right Bde making its main crossing at the Lock in S.1.d. and a subsidiary crossing at the existing wooden bridges in S.7.c. and the Left Bde making its main crossing at the Canal Bend in M.31.central, with a subsidiary crossing about 200 yards N. of this point in M.26.c. Simultaneously with the opening of the barrage No. 1 Special Coy R.E. will put down a smoke barrage immediately E. of the Canal to cover the Infantry crossing.

Artillery and M.G. Barrages will open on the line of the Canal Bank until Zero plus 3 minutes, during which time the storming parties with bridging equipment will close up to the barrage.

The 1st Lift of Artillery barrage will be at Zero plus 3 minutes. Inf. Bdes after establishing crossings will advance direct to the BLUE DOTTED (Bridgehead) Objective under a creeping barrage.

There will be a pause on the BLUE DOTTED Line of 1 hour and a half, during which a portion of the Artillery will move forward.

The advance to the BLUE Line will be continued under a creeping barrage, the Left Bde capturing the RED and RED DOTTED Objectives under the same barrage. After 15 minutes protective barrage on the BLUE Objective on the Right Bde front, two Bdes R.F.A. will come directly under the orders of the B.G.C. 2nd Inf. Bde. This Bde will decide according to circumstances on a Zero hour for the attack on its RED Objective and will arrange its own artillery support as regards attacking FESMY from the N.

The C.R.A. will arrange for an artillery barrage at the Zero hour notified by 2nd Inf. Bde to cover the advance of this Bde on to LA JUSTICE and the RED Objective N. of that place.

9. **Subsidiary Operation by the 3rd Inf. Bde to Capture CATILLON and Form a Bridgehead.**

The attack will be delivered at Zero hour from the S. under enfilade Artillery and M.G. Barrages arranged by B.G.C. 3rd Inf. Bde with Artillery Bde and M.G. Coy at his disposal. One Section of Tanks is placed at disposal of 3rd Inf. Bde to assist in this operation. As soon as CATILLON is cleared this Section will rally and come into Div. Reserve.

/The Task

The task of the 3rd Inf. Bde after clearing CATILLON will be to form a bridgehead and to secure and hold the houses in M.20.a. until touch is obtained with 38nd Div. on Left and 1st Inf. Bde on Right. As the operation progresses the 3rd Inf. Bde will be withdrawn into Reserve and on receipt of orders will withdraw to VAUX ANDIGNY and MOLAIN.

10. During the nights 2/3rd and 3/4th November the Pioneers (1/6th Welch Regt.) assisted troops to entrench themselves in assembly positions.

11. Zero hour was fixed for 05.45 hours.

(d) ACCOUNT OF THE ACTION.

The assembly was completed accurately and troops advanced at Zero in a thick mist, which materially assisted the Infantry approach to the Canal. The assembling troops and bridging parties moved forward close up to the barrage.

(i) On the 1st Inf. Bde front, as soon as the barrage lifted at Zero plus 3 minutes, the four leading bridges were successfully pushed across the Canal and the Infantry immediately started to cross over to the East Bank. Practically no resistance was met with on the West Bank of the Canal except for 1 hostile machine gun, whose team was disposed of by a sergeant of the 23rd Field Coy.

On the East Bank the 1st Loyal North Lancs. met with a certain amount of machine gun fire, but these guns were quickly disposed of by the leading platoon. The 1st Camerons further to the Right crossed without opposition and by Zero plus 20 minutes the whole of the two leading battalions of this Bde had successfully crossed over the Canal - the 23rd Field Coy having succeeded in establishing four bridges across the Canal by 10 minutes after Zero. The hostile artillery barrage which was slow in opening fell in rear of the leading battalions and did no damage.

(ii) On the 2nd Inf. Bde front it had been estimated that if no hitch occurred the bridge over the Lock would be in position by five minutes after Zero, but considerable difficulty was in fact experienced, the stream West of the Lock proving a more formidable obstacle than had been anticipated. During the check which ensued the troops of this Bde came under heavy shell fire. The fine example of the Battalion Comdr., (2/Rl. Sussex) and of the O.C. 409th Field Coy, aided by their officers, however, was paralleled by the resolute bearing of all the troops - the Infantry and R.E. co-operating with the greatest determination - and in spite of M.G. fire from the Lock Houses and from the direction of BOIS de L'ABBAYE, the first bridge was in position across the Canal by twenty five minutes after Zero. A brisk fight ensued at the Lock Houses with the enemy garrison, but this was soon overcome and shortly afterwards the whole of the 2/Rl. Sussex Regt. and a large number of the 2/K.R.R.C. were across and were making for the line of the road in S.2.a. & c. on which our barrage became protective for 20 minutes. On the right of the 2/Rl. Sussex again, one company of the 2/K.R.R.C. had intended to force a subsidiary crossing by using the enemy's existing wooden footbridges across the Reservoir. During the afternoon of the 3rd inst. these footbridges were reported to be badly damaged and the Company of the 2/K.R.R.C. were in consequence provided with Berthen Boats to assist them in crossing the water. On arrival at the footbridge position difficulties were encountered in reaching the Reservoir and it was found impossible to make use of the Berthen Boats, so the Company Comdr. led his men to the Lock Bridge and took his company over in the wake of the remainder of the 2/K.R.R.C.

/Despite

Despite all these checks the units of this Bde on reaching the line of the Road in S.2.a. & c. were able to reorganise and cover their full frontages according to original plan.

By this time both Bdes reported the capture of a large number of prisoners and stated that the opposition met with was considerably less as the approach to the BLUE DOTTED Line was made.

(iii) Simultaneously with the operations of the 1st and 2nd Inf. Bdes the 3rd Inf. Bde carried out the attack on CATILLON. The attack was made from the South and carried out by the 1st Gloucesters, the troops being assembled prior to Zero in the Orchards in R.30.a. Excellent progress was made, although owing to the thick mist it was difficult to keep direction. The Left Coy of the attacking battalion encountered M.Gs. on the S.W. outskirts of the village, but these were soon overcome and progress was continued towards the Church. From this point one of the Tanks which had been detailed to work forward with the 1st Gloucesters rendered valuable assistance in reducing some more M.Gs., forcing the crews to surrender. The Right Coy of the attacking battalion encountered heavy M.G. fire from the hedgerows and orchards, but working round these, eventually, succeeded in capturing 9 or 10 M.Gs. with crews. The Southern portion of the village was now almost cleared of the enemy and the advance was made towards the bridge over the Canal. Another fine assault by one of the Tanks, in co-operation with the Infantry, successfully routed a Heavy M.G. cleverly placed in a house near the Bridge. Meanwhile 2 Coys of the 1st S.Wales Bdrs. approached CATILLON from the West and proceeded to mop up the remainder of the village. These two Coys worked forward in co-operation with a third Coy of the 1st Gloucester Regt. who worked systematically through the village, clearing first the part East of the Church down to the Canal.

During this period a very fine artillery barrage was maintained on the Canal Bank and on this lifting to enable troops to push forward to secure the bridge crossing, fully a hundred Germans scrambled from the remaining cellars and were taken prisoners. Progress over the actual bridge crossings was slow at first, owing to the very difficult obstacle made by piecing together with strong barbed wire entanglements of a large conglomeration of farming implements thrown in a mass into the river. This was, however, successfully manoeuvred and by 08.10 hours six platoons of the 1st Gloucesters were across the Canal and pushing out to form the bridgehead and endeavouring to get touch with neighbouring troops on the right and left.

(iv) The advance of the 1st and 2nd Inf. Bdes to the BLUE LINE was resumed, after 1½ hours halt for re-organization, at Zero plus 229 minutes under cover of an excellent creeping barrage and area shoot. On the 1st Inf. Bde front the 1st Bn. Black Watch moved forward to pass through the 1st Loyal North Lancs and advanced on a three Coy front on the left of the 1st Camerons. Advancing well up behind the barrage the right of the 1st Camerons got forward as far as ROBEL-METRE, where it was held up by very heavy shelling. Meanwhile the Left Coy of this battalion moving round the shelled area reached the road S. of GRAND GALOP Farm and endeavoured to turn a strongly defended position at LA GAMBOTTE. On the Left again the Right Coy of the 1st Black Watch moved through the Southern houses of BOYAU de LEU and advanced to GRAND and PETIT GALOP Farms. M.G. fire from GRAND GALOP Farm held up the advance for a short time, but eventually a party of about 30 Germans tried to get away and gave this Coy possession of the Farm. (Amongst those captured no fewer than 1 Officer and 10 O.R. were in possession of the Iron Cross). The Centre Coy advancing with its Left on the LA GROISE - LANDRECIES Road met little opposition until the houses about M.22.central were reached, but here resistance was encountered and it was not till 12.15 hours that all houses as far as M.22.b.5.7. were finally captured.

/As no signs

As no signs of the troops of the Div. on the left were observed further attempts to advance to M.22.b.9.9. were temporarily abandoned. The Left Coy of this battalion encountered little resistance until reaching MEZIERES. Here the enemy endeavoured to fight, but were caught by surprise, many being killed and over 50 prisoners and a dozen horses being captured. Touch with the L.N.Lancs on the Left again was then gained, one Coy of this battalion having advanced and made good the line of the CATILLON - MEZIERES Road as far East as M.21.b.0.5. and at 17.15 hours touch was established with the Bde on the Left at MALASSISE Farm in M.15.b. and a joint post established at bridge just N. of MEZIERES (M.15.d.8.0.).

Well over 500 prisoners were reported captured up to mid-day by 1st Inf. Bde alone.

(v) On the 2nd Inf. Bde front the 1st Bn. Northamptonshire Regt. (less 1 Coy already in support to the 2/Rl. Sussex) were brought up from Reserve for the attack against FESMY and just prior to the resumption of the new advance one Coy took over from the 2/K.R.R.C. on the PETIT CAMBRESIS - LA GROISE Road (BLUE DOTTED Line) immediately West of FESMY. The remaining Coys of the Northamptons moved up in rear of the two leading battalions. Early reports stated that all four Coys of the 2/Rl. Sussex in line were moving to the BLUE Line in conformity with the 1st Camerons on the Left and 2/K.R.R.C. on the Right. Very few of the enemy were seen and little or no resistance was met with. A cavalry patrol (Royal Scots Greys) was then despatched to reconnoitre the VIELLE - LA JUSTICE Road and gain touch with the enemy. Later reports from this patrol stated they were heavily fired on by machine guns from the Cross Roads and houses at VIELLE and in consequence artillery fire was brought to bear on this village.

Just before mid-day the 46th Div. (In Corps Reserve immediately in rear of 1st Div.) was ordered to move forward one Bde to the MAZING-HEIN - LA LOUVIERE Area, which, on arrival, was to be put at the disposal of the G.O.C. 1st Div. to be used only in case of necessity. Owing to the French troops on the right of the 2nd Inf. Bde being unable to get forward up to time as fast as had been hoped, the 2nd Inf. Bde task, which was already a difficult operation, stood a chance of becoming impossible, in view of the long strung out right flank which it was forced to throw back to protect itself from the gap between its forward position and that of the French. In view of this situation one battalion of the 46th Div. was put at the disposal of the 2nd Inf. Bde to be used in reserve, and orders were then given to 1st Bn. Northamptonshire Regt. to push two Coys Into FESMY, making good to the N. & S. Grid Line through S.10.central, gain touch with the French if possible and push on to the RED Line.

Shortly after mid-day the BLUE LINE N. of FESMY was captured, but the situation at FESMY itself was doubtful. Troops had entered the village but were held up by the Church by M.G. fire. Very little resistance was met with and only slight M.G. fire encountered, and hostile shelling had practically ceased. (Aeroplane reports about this time stated the enemy were seen moving their guns to rear positions). The French made arrangements to attack again at 16.00 hours and endeavour to join hands with the 1st Div. troops at LA JUSTICE. Accordingly the 1st Bn. Northamptonshire Regt. were ordered to suspend operations till 16.00 hours, when they were to go forward with the French supported by 'crashes' of artillery fire, the 2/K.R.R.C. swinging their right to conform. This operation proved entirely successful and on its conclusion the 2nd Inf. Bde Line ran as follows:- From VIELLE Cross Roads, N.W. along HAUTREVE Road to S.4.d.5.8., thence N. to junction with 1st Inf. Bde at M.34.d.6.6., the 1st Northamptonshire Regt. on the right holding a defensive flank between VIELLE Cross Roads and the Canal, enclosing FESMY.

/A patrol.

A patrol of the 1st Bn. Northamptonshire Regt. had penetrated as far as LA JUSTICE taking prisoners, but as the French were only on the Western outskirts of BERGUES and did not propose to enter that village till next morning, it was decided to organise the Bde front on the above line for the night and push on at daybreak, gaining touch with the French at LA JUSTICE.

(e) In view of the very successful advance made during the day the IX Corps decided to resume operations on the next morning, using the 46th Div. to exploit further into the enemy's positions. Orders were issued accordingly for two Bdes to relieve Bdes of the 1st and 32nd Divs. astride the main road, and the 1st Inf. Bde were withdrawn on relief and marched back to MAZINGHIEN - RIBEAUVAL Area. Meanwhile the Bn. of the 46th Div. in reserve to the 2nd Inf. Bde was relieved by the 1/6th Welch Regt. (Pioneers), who came into reserve at L'HERMITAGE. The 2nd Inf. Bde remained in the line and consolidated its gains.

Meanwhile the operations of the 3rd Inf. Bde having been entirely successful, the two battalions in and around CATILLON (1st S.Wales Borderers and 1st Gloucesters) were withdrawn and marched back to the VAUX ANDIGNY - MOLAIN Area. The third battalion of this Bde (2/Welch) remained in line, holding the bank of the Canal N. & S. of PETIT CAMBRESIS, maintaining liaison between the French and 2nd Inf. Bde. The 2/Welch remained throughout the days operations on the West bank of the Canal, but successfully captured the bridge at PETIT CAMBRESIS and cleared the area opposite its front as far as the Canal Bank.

On the morning of the 5th in conjunction with the attack of the 46th Div. patrols of the 1st Northamptonshire Regt. captured LA JUSTICE without opposition, and joined hands with the French at the Farm.

The subsequent advance of the 46th Div. and the French enabled the 2nd Inf. Bde to be squeezed out, and this Bde was accordingly given orders to withdraw to the LA VALLEE MULATRE - WASSIGNY area.

(f) RESULTS OF THE DAY'S OPERATIONS.

As the results of the day's operations the 1st Div. forced the passage of the SAMBRE - OISE Canal, and advanced its line over 4,000 yards on a frontage of 5,000 yards and captured the villages of CATILLON, MEZIERES and FESMY, and the hamlets of LA GROISE, GRAND GALOP, VIEVILLE, de L'ABBAYE, L'ERMITAGE, SANS FOND and ROBELMETRE.

A total of 45 officers and 1540 O.Rs. unwounded and 4 Officers and 109 O.Rs. wounded, through C.C.S., making a total of 49 Officers and 1649 O.Rs. prisoners were captured during the day, together with over 20 guns of various calibres.

The total casualties of the Div. were under 500 in all.

One of the chief causes leading to the very quick and successful crossing of the Canal was the excellent assistance rendered by the 1st Div. Engineers in the design, construction and placing in position of the bridges over which the infantry passed.

Information with regard to the actual details of the Canal was, with the exception of two patrol reports, practically all obtained from air photographs. Although these showed the existence of several footbridges and other means of crossing the Canal used by the enemy, it was not thought advisable to use any of these, especially as they were stated to be prepared for demolition.

The two crossings ultimately decided on were of entirely different natures, i.e. No. 1 over the Lock (2nd Inf. Bde) being a comparatively short span of about 17' with hard abutments, and No. 2 at the Canal Bend (1st Inf. Bde) having a span of over 45' of water with muddy sides, and a masonry wall on the East side certainly, and possibly on the West side as well.

/It was decided

It was decided that the bridges carrying the first wave troops should be carried up bodily as bridges, and that no constructional work should be necessary on arrival. For this, the first wave infantry bridges at the Lock were designed as single span bridges, as light as possible consistent with their being able to support 4 to 6 men on them at one time. They were fitted with a lever and pair of wheels so that they could be launched from the near abutment without requiring anyone on the far side to receive them.

The first wave infantry bridges at Crossing No. 2 were floating bridges carried on German steel floats, of which sufficient were available for 4 bridges and which from their lightness and shape produced the most portable bridge and the one best adapted for sliding over mud. The several bays of each bridge were hinged together in such a way as to give the maximum vertical flexibility, to avoid any difficulty in passing over the Canal banks and the head of each bridge was fitted with a ladder to enable the far bank to be scaled with ease.

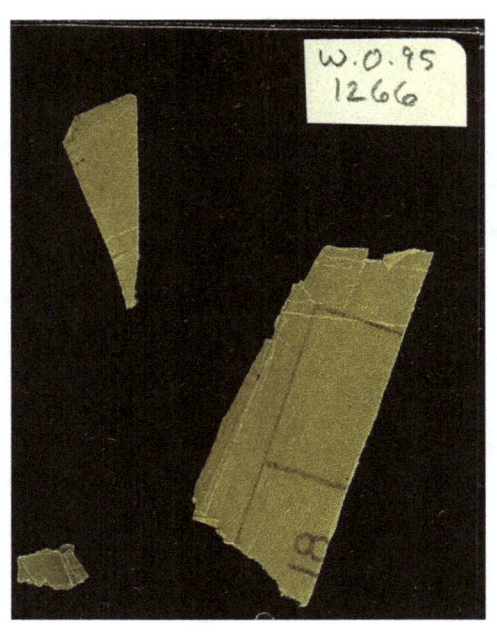

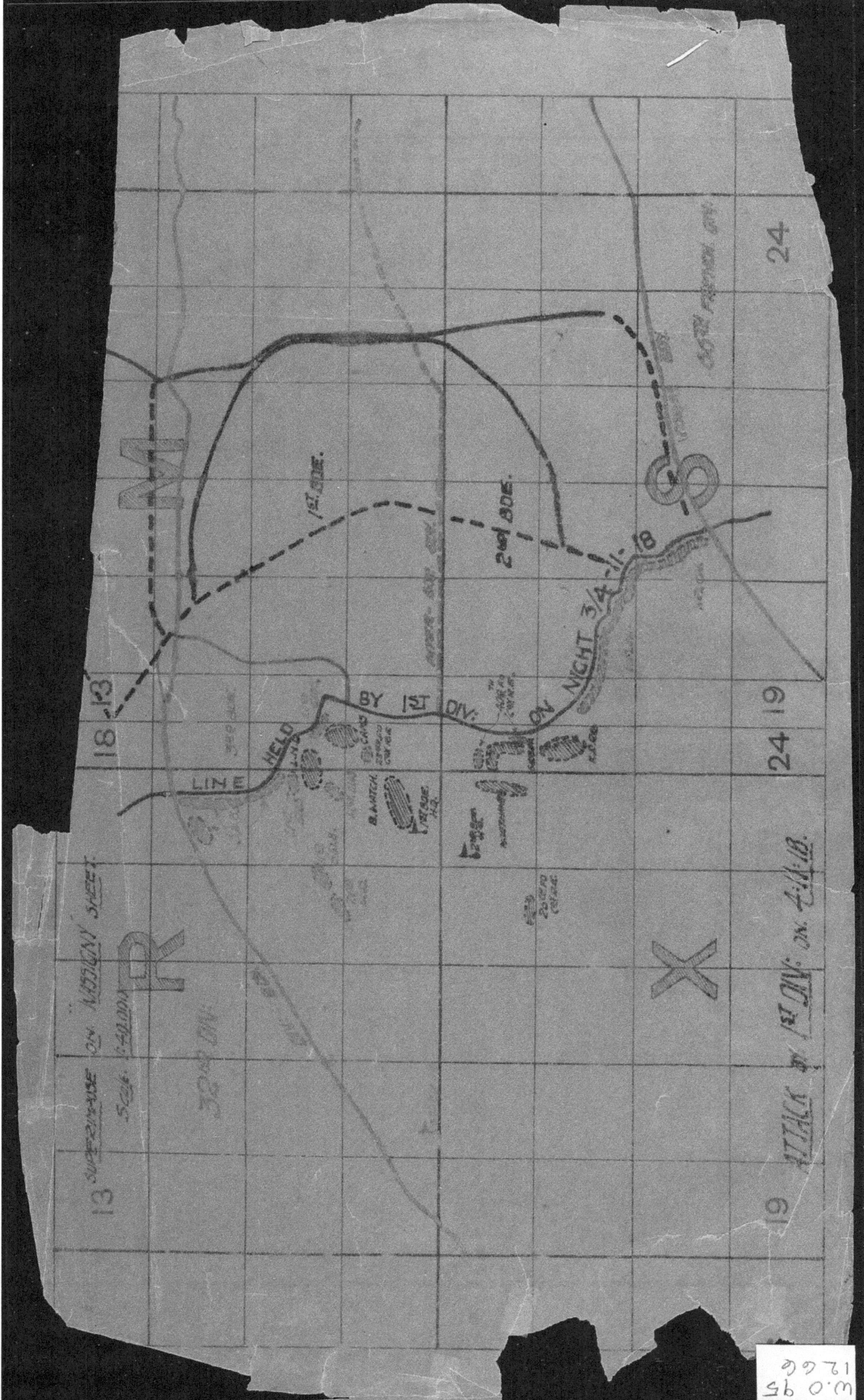

Nº 205. V.7.
SCALE 1:10,000. (APPROX.)
5.

CONFIDENTIAL.

Lieut. Col. R. E. Berkeley, D.S.O.,
    Comdg. 1st L.North Lancs. Regt.

     I wish to express to you personally and to the 1st. Battn. Loyal North Lancashire Regt. my admiration of the completeness of your arrangements for the operation of crossing the SAMBRE Canal and subsequent exploitation on the Eastern side. Your Battalion and the 1st Battn. Cameron Highlanders reached the Eastern bank simultaneously and the complete co-operation which existed was entirely responsible for the success of the operation.

     I congratulate all ranks on their staunch devotion to duty and hope that the 4th November 1918. may be a memorable day in the history of the War and add one more to the gallant record of your Regiment.

                                      L.L.Wheatley.
                                           Brigadier General.

7th. November 1918.
                       Commanding 1st. Infantry Brigade.
            CERTIFIED TRUE COPY.
                                         R.E.Berkeley *Lieut. Col.*
                                        Commdg. 1st Bn. Loyal N. Lancashire Regt.

Army Form C. 2118.

WAR DIARY
or
INTELLIGENCE SUMMARY.

(Erase heading not required.)

Instructions regarding War Diaries and Intelligence Summaries are contained in F. S. Regs., Part II. and the Staff Manual respectively. Title pages will be prepared in manuscript.

December 1918. 1st Bn: The Loyal North Lancashire Regiment. Vol 5 Z Sheet I

Place	Date	Hour	Summary of Events and Information	Remarks and references to Appendices
ONHAYE	1-12-18		Ref Sheets BELGIUM and FRANCE. 1/100,000. NAMUR and MARCHE. GERMANY 1/100,000. 1M.12.2L. The march to the Rhine was resumed. Route lay through DINANT and the Battalion was played past the Divisional Commander by the Divisional Band at the MEUSE was crossed. At a hill, about 6 kilometres, was encountered on the Eastern bank and at the top, the C/O Commander watched the Battalion march past. The Billets in CELLES were reached about 13.30 hrs	JL
CELLES	2-12-18		March resumed. Country gradually getting wilder, and the scenery on the march was superb. The destination CHEVETOGNE was reached about 13 hrs.	JL
CHEVETOGNE	3/12/18 to 8/12/18		The Division halted for a few days. Time was spent in cleaning and Ceremonial Parades. A small meeting was held on the last day. The Colours, for which Lt Heath and 20 other ranks had been sent home, arrived with the Battalion on the 6th and were first carried on a ceremonial parade on the 8th.	JL
CHEVETOGNE	9/12/18		March resumed. For the first time, the weather was bad for the march, and a steady day drizzle set in soon after the start. In spite of the weather and the length of the march (13½ miles), no men fell out, and the Battalion reached billets in BAILLONVILLE and RABOSEE about 14.45 hrs.	JL

Army Form C. 2118.

WAR DIARY
or
INTELLIGENCE SUMMARY.
(Erase heading not required.)

Instructions regarding War Diaries and Intelligence Summaries are contained in F. S. Regs., Part II. and the Staff Manual respectively. Title pages will be prepared in manuscript.

Sheet II

Place	Date	Hour	Summary of Events and Information	Remarks and references to Appendices
BAILLONVILLE.	10/12/18		March resumed. Weather, though threatening, remained fine for the march, and destination, BARVAUX, was reached about 12.30 hours.	
BARVAUX	11/12/18		March resumed. Unfortunately the weather which was fine in the early morning, grew steadily worse, and with a late start (11.10 hours) a very wet march resulted. MORMONT, our destination, was reached about 12.30 hours.	
MORMONT.	12/12/18		Battalion halted for one day.	
	13/12/18		March resumed. A long march, uphill nearly the whole way, to some of the highest ground in BELGIUM. Altitude reached was about 2000 feet, and during the latter half of the march all view was obscured by the low-lying clouds through which the Battalion marched. Destination, ODEIGNE, a small and dilapidated hamlet, was reached about 13.30 hours.	
ODEIGNE.	14/12/18		Another wet march over very high ground. Our destination proved a big improvement on our last billets, and consisted of 3 hamlets of SART, PETIT SART and GRAND SART.	
LES SART	15/12/18		Slight improvement in the weather for our last full days march through BELGIUM, and our destination, COURTIL, was reached without incident.	

Army Form C. 2118.
Sheet III

WAR DIARY
or
INTELLIGENCE SUMMARY.
(Erase heading not required.)

Instructions regarding War Diaries and Intelligence Summaries are contained in F. S. Regs., Part II. and the Staff Manual respectively. Title pages will be prepared in manuscript.

Place	Date	Hour	Summary of Events and Information	Remarks and references to Appendices
COURTIL	16.12.18.		Battalion marched into GERMANY by the ST VITH road with Colours flying. The Divisional Commander witnessed the march past at the Frontier. The day was unfortunately again very wet and squally, which tended to spoil an historic occasion. The last 2 miles of the march were over very bad and muddy roads, and our destination, KRONTBACH, proved a poor and dirty hamlet.	J.
KRONTBACH	17.12.18		After an early start, and a long pull through very muddy side roads, the Battalion regained the main road and after a long march of 13 miles reached our destination MANDERFELD about 14.30 hours, to find that 2 Companies had to march on another 2 miles to billets in BERTERATH.	J.b.
MANDERFELD	18.12.18		The most unpleasant march so far experienced. The weather was very squally and heavy rain and snowshowers and a driving wind soon soaked every man to the skin, and even whilst marching it was hard to keep warm. The inhabitants of our destination DAHLEM were not very well disposed, but eventually all troops were billeted where they were able to dry their clothes.	J.b.

Army Form C. 2118.

WAR DIARY
or
INTELLIGENCE SUMMARY.
(Erase heading not required.)

Sheet IV

Instructions regarding War Diaries and Intelligence Summaries are contained in F. S. Regs., Part II. and the Staff Manual respectively. Title pages will be prepared in manuscript.

Place	Date	Hour	Summary of Events and Information	Remarks and references to Appendices
DAHLEM	19.12.18		A short march and an improvement in the weather. Destination BLANKENHEIMER	
BLANKENHEIM-ERDORF	20.12.18		DORF was reached about 12.00 hours. Day of rest, after 7 days marching, mostly through rain and snow and over poor roads.	J.
"	21.12.18		Commencement of the last period of our march at length brought us to very good billets in MUNSTEREIFEL.	J.
MUNSTEREIFEL	22.12.18		A short march and a lovely sunny day with a touch of frost. Billets in KLUCKENHEIM were reached about 12.00 hours.	J.
KLUCKENHEIM	23.12.18		The end of our march to the Rhine. Unfortunately bad weather and the absence of any kind of a road for 2 miles in the middle of the march made it rather a trying day. Our final destination BORNHEIM was reached about 14.30 hours. Billets were found to be quite good, and the Battalion settled down to enjoy a well earned rest. The Battalion marched for 13 days out of 15 between 9th + 23rd and covered 135 miles. During this period only 2 men fell out behind the Regimental Transport and the total sick admissions from all causes were only 26 OR, inhabit	

1ST BN LOYAL NTH LANCS.
JAN - APR 1919

Army Form C. 2118.

WAR DIARY
or
INTELLIGENCE SUMMARY.
(Erase heading not required.)

1st Battalion The Loyal North Lancashire Regt.
January 1919.

Page 1

Place	Date	Hour	Summary of Events and Information	Remarks and references to Appendices
			Ref: Germany 1/100,000 2.L.	
BORNHEIM	1.1.19		Fine day. Battalion Route march. Part of route lay along foot path by the Rhine. Party of 56 men left the Battalion for Demobilization.	
"	2.1.19 to 5.1.19		Individual Platoon and Company training continued. Most of the time was devoted to steady drill and Ceremonial.	
"	6.1.19		Lt Colonel R.E. Berkeley DSO assumed Command of 1st Infy Bde, and Major Mason MC DCM assumed Command of the Battalion. The following Officers & N.C.O. were mentioned in Despatches" (London Gazette 27th Dec 18) Capt A.B. Bare DSO MC. Capt A.B. Bretton DSO MC. Lieut (A/Capt) W. Roberts. 10025 S/C O'Brien.	
"	7.1.19		Baths were at last established in the Brigade area, and a much needed change of underclothing handed in - the first since the Armistice.	
"	8.1.19 to 10.1.19		Training was entered on some lines as above. Educative training is now in full swing. One morning ten weeks for each Company's and voluntary classes in the evenings between 17.00 and 19.00 hours. About 50-70 men usually avail themselves of the latter opportunities.	
"	11.1.19		Battalion Ceremonial Drill.	

WAR DIARY
or
INTELLIGENCE SUMMARY.
(Erase heading not required.)

Army Form C. 2118.

Place	Date	Hour	Summary of Events and Information	Remarks and references to Appendices
BORNSTEIM	12/1/19 to 14/1/19		Uneventful period. Closing stages of the Inter-Platoon Football Competition were reached.	
"	15/1/19		Brigade Ceremonial Parade in view of expected inspection by the Corps Commander. This was however subsequently cancelled. In the afternoon, the Battalion played the 1st Camerons and were beaten 5-2 after a good fight. As the Battalion had only 1 of our old players left, and the others did not represent the flag, it was considered a very promising performance. Platoon and Company training continued. On 19th the Battalion played 1st The Black Watch but did not show the good form displayed against the Camerons, and after a disappointing game were beaten 3-1.	JL.
"	16/1/19 to 19/1/19			JL.
"	19/1/19 to 29/1/19		Training continued. Weather throughout this period was cold with occasional slight falls of snow. On 22nd the final of the Inter Platoon Football Competition was played off :- No 1 v No 13, resulting in an easy win for No 13 Platoon. 2/Lt Fiddes M.C. rejoined the Battalion. Capt & M. R.K. Rowley joined the Battalion on posting.	JL.
	30/1/19			JL.

Army Form C. 2118.

Sheet III

WAR DIARY
or
INTELLIGENCE SUMMARY.
(Erase heading not required.)

Instructions regarding War Diaries and Intelligence Summaries are contained in F. S. Regs., Part II. and the Staff Manual respectively. Title pages will be prepared in manuscript.

Place	Date	Hour	Summary of Events and Information	Remarks and references to Appendices
BORNHEIM.	31/1/19.		Brigade Cross Country Run of about 3 miles. Battalion finished 8th. the entries were unlimited and teams with first 10 men in to count. 8 competitors from the Battalion had finished when the winners Black watch, got 10 men in next to finish. Effective Strength of the Battalion on this date was: 36 Officers 824 O.R.s.	
"	29/1/19		The 2nd Battalion (81st Foot) having arrived in the area, sent over a party to pay a visit. This included a Football Match, the first in the history of the Regiment after an excellent match, was left drawn at 2 all.	
	3-2-1919			

Major
Cmdg 1st L. N. Lanc. Regt

1st. Brigade No. G. 1/415.

1st. The Black Watch.
1st. L.N. Lancs.
1st. Cameron Hrs.

      Herewith 1 copy of narrative of operations carried out by 1st. Division on 17th, 18th and 19th. Octr. 1919.

      The narrative for the operations from 4th. Novr. is being compiled and will be distributed later.

9th. January 1919.

                                                Captain,
                    Brigade Major, 1st. Infantry Brigade.

NARRATIVE OF OPERATIONS OF 1st DIVISION
on OCTOBER 17th, 18th & 19th
1918.

(a). ORDER OF BATTLE.

    G.O.C. - Major-General E.P.STRICKLAND, C.B., C.M.G., D.S.O.

1st Inf. Bde. (Right Bde.)

    Brigadier-General L.L.WHEATLEY, C.M.G., D.S.O.

        1st Bn. The Black Watch (Royal Highlanders).
        1st Bn. Loyal North Lancs. Regt.
        1st Bn. Queens Own Cameron Highlanders.
        1st Trench Mortar Battery.
Attached.
        1 Sqdn Royal Scots Greys.
        Coy. 1st Bn. M.G.C.
        1 Section 23rd Field Coy.

2nd Inf. Bde. (Left Bde.)

    Brigadier-General G.C.KELLY, D.S.O.

        2nd Bn. Rl. Sussex Regt.
        1st Bn. Northamptonshire Regt.
        2nd Bn. Kings Royal Rifle Corps.
        2nd Trench Mortar Battery.
Attached.
        1 Sqdn. Royal Scots Greys.
        Coy. 1st Bn. M.G.C.
        12 Whippet Tanks of No. 6. Bn. Tank Corps.
        No. 1. Section No. 16 Bn. Tank Corps.
        1 Section 409th Field Coy.

/ Artillery

(2).

Artillery.

   C.R.A. - Brigadier-General H.F.E.LEWIN, C.M.G.

    25th Bde. R.F.A.) 1st Div.Artillery.
    39th Bde. R.F.A.)

Attached.
    5th Army Bde.R.H.A.
    "T" Battery R.H.A.
    298th Army Bde.R.F.A.

In Reserve.
    3rd Infantry Bde.
    23rd Field Coy (less 1 Section).
    409th Field Coy (less 1 Section).
    26th Field Coy.
    1/6th Welch Regt.(Pioneers).
    1st Bn.M.G.C. (less 2 Coys).

(b). DISPOSITIONS.

   Detailed dispositions of troops at Zero are shewn on map attached.

Headquarters.
Adv.Div.H.Q.	D.9.b.3.9.
Rear Div.H.Q.	BRANCOURT.
Div.Arty.	D.9.b.3.9.
Right Group R.F.A.	W.19.a.7.7.
Left Group R.F.A.	W.19.a.7.7.
D.E.	D.9.b.3.9.
Right Inf.Bde.	W.19.a.7.7.
Left Inf.Bde.	W.19.a.7.7.
Reserve Inf.Bde.	FRIACOURT FARM in C.17.Central.

(c). **BRIEF PLAN OF THE OPERATIONS.**

The general plan of the operations is explained by the following extracts from 1st Div. Battle Instructions :-

"IX Corps is attacking on a date "Z" which has been given out verbally. II American Corps and XV French Corps will be attacking on Left and Right respectively.
Attached map shews First Objectives RED DOTTED, Second Objective RED, Third Objective GREEN.
On the Corps front the RED DOTTED Objective is being taken by 46th Div. on the Right and 6th Div. on the Left. Inter-Divl. Boundary is shewn on the map.
The 1st Div. will pass through the 6th Div. on the RED DOTTED line and capture the RED and GREEN Objectives.

GENERAL STAGES OF 1st DIV. OPERATIONS.
There will be a halt in the barrage of ½ an hour on the RED DOTTED line. The heads of attacking Inf. Bdes. will then pass through 6th Div. and capture RED objective under a creeping barrage.
There will be a halt of 3 hours on the RED line while Artillery and M.Gs move forward. Attacking Inf. Bdes. will then advance under a creeping barrage and capture GREEN objective.
Attacking Inf. Bdes. will exploit success towards the Canal de la SAMBRE.

The following troops will be operating under the orders of G.O.C. 1st Div. :-

(a). **Detachment of 5th Cav. Bde** under Lt.-Col. McCOMBIE, O.C. Royal Scots Greys (present H.Q. BOHAIN D.14.a.6.9).   Composition - 3 Squadrons (each less 1 Troop)
Royal Scots Greys.
"E" Battery R.H.A.
5th Cav. Bde. M.G. Squadron
(12 M.Gs).

(b). No.6 Bn. Tank Corps consisting of 12 Whippet Tanks. O.C. Lt.-Col. SOMERS - present H.Q. ELLINCOURT.

(c). 1 Section "B" Coy. No. 16 Bn. Tank Corps consisting of 1 Male and 2 Female Mark V Tanks under Captain CHICK - present H.Q. PONCHAUX.
(N.B. The remaining 3 Sections of this Coy. are co-operating in the first instance with 6th and 46th Divs. They are going to rally after capture of RED DOTTED Line and such as are fit for further action, will then co-operate with 1st Div.).

/ Action of attacking........
P.T.O.

(2).

Action of Attacking Bdes.

(a). Dividing line between Right and Left Bdes. will be an E. and W. line through ANGIN FARM as far East as railway in W.23.c.8.0 and thence the railway to F.3.c. central.

After capture by Left Bde. of WASSIGNY Right Bde. will be prepared on receipt of orders from Div. H.Q. to take over the front on the GREEN objective as far North as road junction in X.21.d.5.3. During further exploitation Inter-Bde Boundary would then be the road from X.21.d.5.3 to S.19.d.0.0.

(b). Both attacking Bdes will arrange for the troops detailed to capture the RED line to follow the attacking Bdes of the 6th Div. and to leap-frog on the RED DOTTED Line during the ½ hour halt on that line.

Bdes will be represented at the Double Bde. H.Q. of 6th Div. at QUARRY W.19.a. from Zero hour onwards. As soon as their troops have leap-frogged, Bdes will establish their H.Q. at this QUARRY which 6th Div. Bdes. are arranging then to vacate.

(c). For the capture of the RED line the Left Bde. will employ a Section of Mark V Tanks attached to it in attacking LA VALLEE MULATRE.

One Female Tank of this Section will operate South of the Railway in Right Bde. area for this purpose.

(d). After the capture of RED line, guns and M.Gs will be moved forward under Div. arrangements to be notified separately to provide a barrage under which Bdes. will each attack and capture the GREEN line. The latter line has been marked arbitrarily on the map by a Grid line. In practice it will be amended to run from North to South as follows :-

In touch with 27th American Div. on the forward slopes of the Spur in X.4.c. - North of road from MAZINGHIEN to REJET-de-BEAULIEU, thence WOOD FARM to X.15.d.0.0 to road junction at X.22.c.2.5 to Road Fork F.3.c.4.8 thence as shown on map.

(e). Co-operation by Mark V Tanks for the capture of GREEN objective will depend on numbers available after preliminary phases of battle. A forecast of possibilities in this respect will be notified later when details of the action of Tanks with 6th and 46th Divs. are ascertained.

/ (f). If sufficient ....

(3).

(f). If sufficient Heavy Tanks are not available, Left Bde will arrange to use 1 Section of Whippets for capture of GREEN objective. Otherwise, Whippet Tanks will be kept for exploitation.

(g). **Exploitation East of GREEN Line.**
No exploitation by Right Bde. nor relief by this Bde. of the Left Bde. in front of WASSIGNY will take place without orders from Div. H.Q. These orders will depend on the progress of the French attack South of the FORET D'ANDIGNY towards HANNAPPES.
If ordered to do so, the Right Bde. will be prepared to exploit Eastwards in touch with Left Bde.
The Left Bde. after capture of GREEN objective will exploit as far East as possible towards the Canal de SAMBRE. If Right Bde. is not ordered to exploit, the Left of the Left Bde. will only be able to get forward, securing, in the first instance, the high ground N.E. of REJET-de-BEAULIEU about X.5.central.

(h). For this exploitation, each Inf. Bde. will have 1 Bde. of Div. Artillery under its direct orders and there will be a Bde. R.G.A. (2 Btys 6" Hows., 2 Btys 60-pdrs) under C.R.A. co-operating.

(i). Bdes. will be prepared to move H.Q. in bounds as follows :-

After capture of WASSIGNY to N. of LA VALLEE MULATRE (approximately W.24.a.). During exploitation to N.W. of WASSIGNY (approximately X.20.c.).

Div. Reserves. (less R.E. & Pioneers).

Orders for all moves will be issued by Div. H.Q. The following forecast is issued for guidance :-

1st Bound - (During 3 hour halt on RED Line) to Valleys S. and S.E. of VAUX ANDIGNY (B.G.C. 3rd Inf. Bde. and O.C. R. Scots Greys at Adv. Div. H.Q.).

2nd Bound - (After capture of WASSIGNY) to Valleys just W. and S. of LA VALLEE MULATRE (B.G.C. 3rd Inf. Bde. and O.C. R. Scots Greys at Double Bde. H.Q. in W.24.a. in touch with B.Gs.C. Right and Left Bdes., and in communication with Div. H.Q. through their communications). "

/2. When the above .....

(4).

2.   When the above instructions were issued the 1st Div. was in Corps Reserve in an area around BELLENGLISE, the Corps front East of BOHAIN being held by 46th Div. on the Right and 6th Div. on the Left.

3.   On the 16th instant, the Div. marched to an area N. and N.W. of BOHAIN, Div. H.Q. moving to BRANCOURT. Inf. Bns. each marched between 11 and 13 miles this day arriving at their destinations in the early afternoon. The 1st and 2nd Inf. Bdes. who were to attack on the 17th on the Right and Left respectively, moved off about midnight for a further march of 2 or 3 miles to their assembly areas.

4.   The arrangements for the assembly of these Bdes. presented some difficulty. Both Bdes. had, according to the plan of operations, to leap-frog troops of the 6th Div. on an objective line 2,500 to 3,000 yards East of VAUX ANDIGNY. As the pause of the barrage on this objective line was only ½ an hour, it was necessary to arrange that the Bdes. should follow the troops of the 6th Div. closely from Zero hour without attempting to wait for information as to the success or failure of the 6th Div. attack. To follow the 6th Div. it was therefore necessary to assemble in the dark immediately in rear and in touch with them.

The attack of the 6th Div. and of the 46th Div. on its Right both debouched however, from the neighbourhood of VAUX ANDIGNY, the 6th Div. attacking East and S.E., the 46th Div. attacking S.E.

The tails of these 2 Divs. therefore converged about VAUX ANDIGNY. In addition to this, the direction of the American attack on the Left of the 6th Div. was considerably North of East. The tail therefore, of the 59th American Bde. which attacked and the head of the 60th American Bde. which was to follow it and leap-frog on the RED line, had both to be in the area just West of VAUX ANDIGNY. This area just west of VAUX ANDIGNY therefore, was required by troops of all 4 Divs. concerned. The major part of the area consisted of a Wood to further complicate matters. Luckily, the wood was chiefly low scrub and the undergrowth was not very thick but even then it was an unpleasant obstacle for night work. All difficulties were overcome, however, by the arrangements made by the 1st and 2nd Inf. Bdes., the 1st Inf. Bde. having to pass through the tail of the 46th Div. before they got in touch with the tail of the Right Bde. of the 6th Div. which they had to follow.

Zero hour was fixed for 05.20 hours.

(d.) Account of........

(d). ACCOUNT OF THE ACTION.

" Assembly was completed accurately and troops advanced at Zero. Unfortunately, however, there was a dense fog from dawn up till about 10.00 hours. The 2nd Inf. Bde. on the Left were unable to find the tracks through Gardens and hedges etc., which they had reconnoitred in order to avoid the main road through VAUX ANDIGNY and the troops were therefore led forward on this road. The enemy concentrated all his Artillery on to VAUX ANDIGNY and on to the Battery areas about BECQUINY. It was therefore, through a heavily shelled area and in a dense fog that the 2 Bdes. had to advance and get in touch with the tail of the 6th Div; the latter in their advance in the fog passed through a lot of M.G. nests unnoticed with the result that both the 1st and 2nd Inf. Bdes., as soon as they got East of VAUX ANDIGNY, were engaged by enemy M.G. fire 2,000 yards before they got to what should have been their forming-up line.

The detailed account of what happened in these circumstances could not be compressed into a short account, but the outstanding feature of the operations is that in spite of the difficulties stated above and the fact that every unit moved throughout with nothing to guide it but a compass bearing, the 4 leading Bns. maintained their cohesion and direction and reached the RED DOTTED line practically on time. This in itself, constitutes a very great military achievement on the part of the units concerned.

Certain instances during this period must be recorded.

The L.N.Lancs took BELLEVUE 500 yards S.E. of VAUX ANDIGNY and 2,000 yards West of the RED DOTTED line where strong enemy M.G. positions threatened to stop all operations in their neighbourhood. This Bn. in its further advance pushed its Right forward into ANDIGNY-les-FERMES in its efforts to get touch with the 46th Div. on its Right and actually took this village.

On the Left of the L.N.Lancs the 1st Cameron Hrs. were at one time completely held up by M.Gs about the RED DOTTED line. The situation here was retrieved by the action of a single platoon despatched by the Bn. Commander to work round by the Railway on the Left and come up behind the enemy's positions. The task which was very brilliantly carried out met with complete success. Another feature in this action, was the close support of a Section of 18-pdrs. working with this Bn.

On the Left of the 2nd Inf. Bde. the 2nd K.R.R.C. were very heavily shelled in VAUX ANDIGNY and on emerging from the village the Bn. Commander and Adjutant found themselves alone with a handful of men, in the fog with the rest of the Bn. apparently lost.

/ within a short space ....
P.T.O.

Within a short space of time, however, the whole Bn. found its way to its correct position and then proceeded to advance still on compass bearings towards the RED line. Up to 4 or 5 hours after Zero this Bn. saw nothing to indicate that there were any troops either on its Right or its Left and during this period, had to fight its way forward against M.G. opposition. When the fog lifted the Bn. found the 1st Northamptonshire Regt. on its Right, in the position it should have been in.

The performance of the latter Regt. was just as creditable as that of the other three mentioned above.

All four Bns. advanced from the RED DOTTED Line towards the RED; on the Right this advance was made at approximately the time table time; on the Left it was somewhat delayed. Very shortly all Bns. however, lost the barrage but in spite of this, units fought their way forward for about 1,000 yards which took the Right of the Div. to its RED objective; the centre past LA VALLEE MULATRE; and the Left to about mid-way between the RED DOTTED and RED Lines to the neighbourhood of the WASSIGNY - ST. SOUPLET Railway.

The feature of this stage of the operations was the close support of the Section of Artillery accompanying Bn. H.Q. on the front of the 1st Cameron Highlanders South of LA VALLEE MULATRE and also the capture of LA VALLEE MULATRE by the 1st Northamptonshire Regt. Against the latter the enemy delivered a counter-attack from the Wood S.E. of the village and succeeded in driving our troops back to the centre of the village.

About midday the general situation was as follows :-

The 46th Div. had established themselves on the RED DOTTED Line from ANDIGNY-les-FERMES inclusive Westwards; the 6th Div. were consolidating on the approximate line of the RED DOTTED Line from ANDIGNY-les-FERMES Northwards just West of LA VALLEE MULATRE; the 1st Div. having passed through the 6th Div., were on an approximate line from F.5.central through the centre of LA VALLEE MULATRE to the Railway in W.18.a. where touch was obtained with the Americans. By this time the barrage was over and any further progress would be dependent on units fighting their way forward with Inf. weapons and such Artillery support as could be arranged by Officers on the spot. The enemy had fought and were continuing to fight well and the prospect of any appreciable advance in these circumstances, was slight. It was therefore decided to organise a barrage for the evening and to make a further organised attack on both Bde fronts.

This attack took place at 17.15 hours the Artillery getting about 2½ hours notice. This was not really sufficient in view of the fact that all the guns had moved during the morning and communications were slow.

/ The barrage therefore ....

The barrage therefore was only moderate. The result of the attack was that on the Right Bde. front the L.N.Lancs and Cameron Hrs. reached the edge of the Wood S.E. of LA VALLEE MULATRE but a counter-preparation by the enemy of gas shell in this area, forced Commanders on the spot to decide to withdraw practically to the line of departure; opposite LA VALLEE MULATRE, the 1st Northamptonshire Regt. again cleared the village and established themselves well East of it; North of them a certain amount of progress was made, troops at one time reaching the vicinity of BELLEVUE; the enemy M.Gs in the neighbourhood of the latter place in the hedges and enclosures there, prevented us maintaining all our gains.

The situation at night was as indicated by the Yellow Line on the attached map.

During the afternoon it was decided that it would not be feasible to make a set piece attack with a barrage until a late hour the next morning as it would be necessary to ascertain definitely during the night, the exact situation of all troops and to give facilities in daylight for the reconnaissance of a definite kicking-off line for the troops detailed to undertake any further attack.

The Americans on the Left decided to attempt an attack at dawn but with the approval of the Corps the Div. insisted that a set piece attack before late in the forenoon was impossible. The Right of the Americans therefore did not attack but decided to conform to our movements later.

The 3rd Inf. Bde. in Reserve moved during the night from the Valley S.W. of VAUX ANDIGNY (to which it and the Reserve Cav.Sqdn. had moved about noon on the 17th) to the valley just West of LA VALLEE MULATRE where it arrived at dawn and Unit Commanders reconnoitred forward in view of a probable attack.

The details of this attack were settled by the Divl. Comdr. at a Conference at Bde. H.Q. at 06.30 hours and an attack was launched at 11.30 hours by the 3rd Inf. Bde. on the left passing through the 2nd Inf. Bde. and by the Reserve Bn. (1st Black Watch) of the 1st Inf. Bde. on the Right. The barrage was put down on the North and South grid line between W.24. and X.19. and rolled due East at 100 yards in 4 minutes.

Arrangements were made with the R.A.F. to smoke the ridge between WASSIGNY and RIBEAUVILLE during the approach march of the 3rd Inf. Bde. to assembly position (the weather which was very thick for fighting prevented this being carried out but the same reason, however, rendered the smoke unnecessary).

When the attack was planned no accurate forecast could be made of the action of the neighbouring Divs. and arrangements were therefore made so that the Divl. operation should be independent of them.

/ To this end ....

P.T.O.

To this end the 1st Inf. Bde. on the Right who were launching the 1st Black Watch to capture WASSIGNY, arranged that the 1st Cameron Highrs should throw a defensive flank back on the North edge of the FOREST D'ANDIGNY.

On the Left the 3rd Inf. Bde. arranged to throw a defensive flank from North of BELLEVUE South of RIBEAUVILLE to the objective line of the RIBEAUVILLE - WASSIGNY Road in X.14.b.

On the Left this defensive flank was required throughout the day; on the Right however, the French South of the 46th Div. made such good progress through the FOREST D'ANDIGNY that by midday, they and troops of the 46th Div. had cleared the FOREST as far East as about a Grid Line between F.7 and 8 and during the afternoon they cleared the FOREST completely.

Meanwhile, the attack of the 1st and 3rd Inf. Bdes. was completely successful, the objectives WASSIGNY and the line of the road from WASSIGNY to RIBEAUVILLE through X.21 - 15 and 14 being all captured (1st Black Watch of the 1st Inf. Bde. on the Right, 2nd Welch and 1st S. Wales Bords. on the 3rd Inf. Bde. front with 1st Glosters forming the defensive flank).

Shortly after nightfall, 1st Black Watch got touch with the 126th French Div. at BLOCUS-d'en-BAS S.E. of WASSIGNY squeezing out the head of the 46th Div. which then passed into Corps Reserve and also releasing the 1st Cameron Hrs. from any duties on the Southern defensive flank.

Meanwhile, on the Left the defensive flank S. of RIBEAUVILLE was maintained by the Reserve Bn. (1st Glosters) of the 3rd Inf. Bde. until nightfall. The Glosters were then ordered to push forward into RIBEAUVILLE which was occupied without opposition though under shell-fire. American troops came up later and took over the village, the 1st Glosters remaining there until touch between the S. Wales Borderers and the Americans was obtained at 23.00 hours.

Useful work was done this day by the 2 Squadrons of the Royal Scots Greys one of which was attached to each attacking Inf. Bde. The squadron on the right did valuable patrol work, ascertaining the position of the French in the afternoon in ANDIGNY FOREST and also reconnoitring to BLOCUS-en-BAS East of the FOREST. The Left Squadron attempted to push out beyond the 3rd Inf. Bde. objective to F^me du BOIS de RIBEAUCOURT but was stopped by enemy M.Gs and the nature of the country which was very close and intersected with hedges. The Squadron nevertheless, did valuable patrolling and inter-communication work.

On the morning of the 19th the advance was resumed by both Bdes. at dawn in a very thick fog which made inter-communication and maintenance of touch between units very difficult. The 3rd Inf. Bde. advanced in 2 bounds meeting with slight opposition and secured the line of the road from PETIT CAMBRESIS to REJET-de-BEAULIEU (the Americans had during the night and in the

/ early morning.......

early morning captured MAZINGHIEN on our Left without opposition). The 3rd Inf. Bde. for these operations were reinforced by the Reserve Squadron Royal Scots Greys and these 2 Squadrons attempted to make the line of the Canal. The nature of the country however, was all against them but their co-operation was invaluable in maintaining touch between the smaller Inf. Units which were operating on very wide fronts. Cavalry patrols enabled us also to find out that the Canal crossings were destroyed and that the enemy still had a few posts this side of the Canal.

Meanwhile, on the Right, the 1st Black Watch of the 1st Inf. Bde. advanced in touch with the 3rd Inf. Bde. about an hour earlier than the French on their Right commenced to advance. This Bn. captured F^{me} de L'ARROUAISE and later obtained touch with the French about this FARM.

The patrol of the Scots Greys with the 1st Inf. Bde. cleared up the situation about OISY where the French had penetrated into the Western outskirts and reported that the bridge was destroyed and that the Germans were in the Eastern edge of the Village. The 1st Inf. Bde. maintained touch between the French and 3rd Inf. Bde. until liaison was established by the 2nd Welch Regt. with the French at the Crucifix N. of OISY on the Inter-Divl. Boundary.

The 1st Inf. Bde. was then squeezed out and came into Divl. Reserve.

This completed the whole task set to the Div. on the 17th instant.

A feature of the operations not mentioned in the account above, was the excellent work done by M.Gs of the 1st Bn. M.G.C. in particularly in regard to the organisation of barrages for the various attacks.

These were especially successful on the morning of the 18th when 48 guns from the high ground N. of LA VALLEE MULATRE fired barrages onto WASSIGNY and the neighbourhood of LA REGET. These were most effective and were much appreciated by the Infantry.

The casualties of the Div. during the period 17th to 18th October were :-

```
Killed   -  11 Officers, 86 Other Ranks.
Wounded  -  35 Officers, 476 Other Ranks.
Missing  -  2 Officers, 54 Other Ranks.
```

/ Captures in prisoners ....
P.T.O.

Captures in Prisoners and Material were :-

Prisoners -
    Unwounded - 31 Officers, 549 Other Ranks.
    Wounded   - 8 Officers, 206 Other Ranks.

Material -

    Field Guns 32
    4.2" Hows. 3
    4.2" H.V. Guns. 2
    6-pdr. A.T. Guns 2
    Machine Guns 160
    Trench Mortars - Heavy... 2
    Trench Mortars - Various. 6
    Bomb Throwers.. 2

* *

Army Form C. 2118.

WAR DIARY

February 1919.   1st Battalion
INTELLIGENCE SUMMARY. The Loyal North Lancashire Regt.
(Erase heading not required)   Part I

Place	Date	Hour	Summary of Events and Information	Remarks and references to Appendices
BORNHEIM	1-2-19 to 4-2-19	Reported Gunning Sheet 2.L.1/40,000.	Cold and frosty weather, but always overcast. Company training continued. Owing to the state of the ground, games were rather at a standstill. On the 4th, the one victory in the Brigade Association Football League was scored at the expense of No.1. Field Ambulance by 6-1. Regimental Trials were started to select Hockey, Rugger and Boxing teams.	JF
"	5-2-19 to 10-2-19.		The weather improved greatly; hard frosts at nights were ended fine sunny days. A certain amount of shooting became available afloat in the grounds of Brigade Head Quarters. Other forms of sport had to be suspended, owing to the frost bound state of the ground.	JF
"	11-2-19 to 13-2-19.		Finals heats of the Brigade Tug of War were held. The Battalion had to pull the 1st Camerons in both the Catch weight & 110 stone & Under Competitions. In the former the Camerons gained as easy victory, but, in the latter, the Battalion team put up a very good pull. Three days later the Cameron team easily defeated the Black Watch in the Brigade Finals.	JF
"	14-2-19		A rapid thaw set in and ground was quickly rendered fit for play. Officers team were defeated at Hockey by the Officers 1st Camerons 4-2.	JF

Army Form C. 2118.

WAR DIARY
or
INTELLIGENCE SUMMARY.
(Erase heading not required.)

Sheet 2.

Instructions regarding War Diaries and Intelligence Summaries are contained in F.S. Regs., Part II. and the Staff Manual respectively. Title pages will be prepared in manuscript.

Place	Date	Hour	Summary of Events and Information	Remarks and references to Appendices
BORNHEIM	15-2-19 to 20-2-19		Dull rainy weather set in, which greatly interfered with the Battalion training. On the 19th, the Corps Commander visited the area, but did not come to the Battalion, as it was extended.	
"	21-2-19		The first round of the Brigade Hockey Competition was played off between the Battalion and 1st Bn Black Watch. This resulted in another win to the Battalion by 3 goals to 1.	
"	22-2-19		The Brigade Boxing Tournament was held in ROISDORF. Gun run of misfortune attended to have been temporarily suspended, and the Battalion boxers put up good fights, securing two 1st places and two second places out of the 6 events.	
"	23-2-19 to 26-2-19		Weather still very unsettled. On the 26th inst, Lt. Colonel R.E. Berkeley, DSO re-assumed command of the Battalion on the return of Brigadier General Wheatley CMG DSO from leave. A small race meeting open only to units of 1st & 2nd Inf. Bdes Groups was held on 23rd. Gun horses entered only for flat races, did not shine and secured only 2 second places in the Company Cmdrs and Consolation events.	
"	27-2-19		Finals of the Divisional Football, Tug of War (2 Weights) and Boxing were held in BONN. In the two former, 1st Bn Cameron Highlanders secured first(sic)	

WAR DIARY or INTELLIGENCE SUMMARY

Army Form C. 2118.

Place	Date	Hour	Summary of Events and Information	Remarks and references to Appendices
			first place. In the latter, boxes of 1st Bde failed rather badly. The two Battalion boxes were knocked out in the early rounds, and every one event was placed to the credit of the Brigade by a brace of 1st Bn. The Bands Match. After the stunts, a farewell dinner was held, also in Bonn, for Officers of the Division. During the day, information was received that the Battalion detailed to relieve us in the Army of the Rhine was due to arrive on the following day, prior to our return to England for reconstruction.	
BORNHEIM	2.3.19		Our relief, 1/7th Battalion The Cheshire Regiment duly arrived and were accommodated partly in BORNHEIM and partly in BRENIG. Pending our departure Major S Mann MC DCM left the Battalion to assume temporary command of 1/6th Battalion The Cheshire Regiment. (O-in-c.) The effective strength of the Battalion in Germany on this date was:— 32 Officers. 641. Other Ranks.	

2-3-19.

W Barkeley, Lieut. Col.
Commdg. 1st Bn. Loyal N. Lancashire Regt.

WAR DIARY
or
INTELLIGENCE SUMMARY

Army Form C. 2118.

1st Bn.
The Loyal North Lancashire Regt
Sheet 1.

March 1919

Place	Date	Hour	Summary of Events and Information	Remarks and references to Appendices
BORNHEIM	1-3-19		Demobilisation re-commenced for all men not liable for retention in the Armies of Occupation.	
"	2-3-19		Regimental transport was withdrawn complete and handed over to the 52nd Bedfords of 34th Division.	
"	3-3-19 to 6-3-19		Demobilisation continued at a steady rate. Prior to the "break-up" of the Battalion, 52 recruits had been obtained for the "Post Bellum", a number comparatively in excess of that found by any other Battalion of 12th Brigade. All mobilization equipment other than that carried on the man was withdrawn and handed over to 52nd Bedfords.	
"	7-3-19		All Officers and men liable for retention in the Army of Occupation on the RHINE left the Battalion to join the 12th Battalion The Loyal North Lancashire Regiment in BONN. Total marching out strength of the draft was 11 Officers and 272 O.R. Total number posted 21 Officers 313 O.Rs. In addition to this, another large dispersal draft was sent off, the effect of which was to reduce the Battalion to 9 Officers and 103 men, composed of Battalion Cadre, details awaiting Demobilisation, men re-enlisted awaiting final approval, and men ear-marked for duty with No 1. T.M.B. when the Battalion is reformed.	
"	8-3-19		The Battalion was reformed into a composite Company under the command of Capt C.S. McCrum M.C.	

Army Form C. 2118.
Sheet 2

WAR DIARY
or
INTELLIGENCE SUMMARY.
(Erase heading not required.)

Place	Date	Hour	Summary of Events and Information	Remarks and references to Appendices
BORNHEIM	9-3-19 to 16-3-19		A dull week spent awaiting orders to proceed home. Details left were gradually sorted out and dispatched to their destinations. On the 10th, a Regimental dinner was held in Bonn at which representatives of the following Battalions were present:- 1st, 2nd, 2/4th, 3/5 & 12th. On 14th, the semi-finals of the Corps Soccer were played, when the 1st Division (1st Cameron Hrs.) beat 6th Division by 1-0. Owing to the reconstitution of the Division forming the Army of the RHINE, the 1st Division ceased to exist on March 15th, and was renamed the WESTERN DIVISION.	JS
BORNHEIM	17-3-19 to 24-3-19		Move orders still failed to materialise. Camerons continued their successful career, winning the final of the Corps Competition v. Corps Troops and also preliminary and semi-finals of Army Commanders Cup Competition. Few remaining details were gradually dispersed.	JS
BORNHEIM	25.3/19 to 31.3/19		First Cadres to leave the Division (2nd Welch & 1st S.W.B.) proceeded back to France prior to embarkation. 1st Cameron Highlanders won the Army Commanders Cup, defeating 8th Bn. Black Watch by 2-1 after an exciting game. Strength of Battalion on 31st inst was :- 6 Officers 68. O.R.	JS

31.3/19.

R.V.Dunsden.
Lieut. Col.
Comndg. 1st Bn. Loyal N. Lancashire Regt.

SECRET.

> 1st BATTALION,
> THE LOYAL NORTH
> LANCASHIRE REGIMENT.
> No.............
> Date...22-4-19.

D.A.G.

GHQ. 3rd Echelon.

In accordance with Demobilisation Regulations, attached please find War Diary for this Battalion for period 1st April 1919 up to date of Embarkation of Cadre, 16th April. 1919.

Please acknowledge receipt.

Hindsell Capt & Adjt

for
Lieut. Col.
Commdg. 1st Bn. Loyal N. Lancashire Regt.

Preston.
22/4/19.

Army Form C. 2118.

WAR DIARY
or
INTELLIGENCE SUMMARY.
(Erase heading not required.)

April 1919

1st Battalion
The Loyal North Lancashire Regt.

Instructions regarding War Diaries and Intelligence Summaries are contained in F. S. Regs., Part II. and the Staff Manual respectively. Title pages will be prepared in manuscript.

Place	Date	Hour	Summary of Events and Information	Remarks and references to Appendices
BORNHEIM.	1-4-19 to 8-4-19		On 3/4 inst. information was received that the Cadre would entrain for DUNKIRK on 13th inst. From CologNE, and on the same day the last remaining details were despatched to Concentration Camps. The weather had been very cold, with frequent snow showers, at length became more seasonable.	
BORNHEIM.	9-4-19 to 12-4-19		All preparations for departure completed. Preparations for the Officers Mess were inadvertently upset by burglars who broke into the Mess Billets on night 11th/12th, and stole most of the food supply!	J.L.
BORNHEIM	13-4-19		The Battalion Cadre entrained at BORNHEIM at 06.00 hours, and arrived at COLOGNE Station by 07.15. Entrainments was completed by 08.00 hours and, at 09.00 hours, the journey to DUNKIRK commenced. DUNKIRK was reached about 22.30 hours on 14th inst, and the remainder of the night was spent in the train.	J.L.
	14/4/19			J.L.
DUNKIRK	15-4-19		The Cadre first proceeded to A Camp, where all men were given baths and clothing disinfected, after which, a further move took place to No. 2. Embarkation Camp. Shortly after our arrival in the latter orders were received that the Cadre would embark for England on the following day. (Destination Depôt PRESTON, and port of disembarkation DOVER.)	J.L.

Army Form C. 2118.

WAR DIARY
or
INTELLIGENCE SUMMARY.
(Erase heading not required.)

Place	Date	Hour	Summary of Events and Information	Remarks and references to Appendices
Dunk. B.C.	16-4-19	at 07.45 hours the Battalion paraded, and marched down to the Docks. Embarkation was completed by 07.30 hours and at 09.45 hours the Battalion sailed from France after 4 years and 8 months on active service. Strength of the Cadre on Embarkation was:— 4* Officers 54 O.R. (* 1 Officer was temporarily detained in Dunkirk on duty, rejoining the Cadre at PRESTON three days later.)	

21-4-19

R V Berkeley Lt. Colonel
Cmdg 1st Loyal N. Lancs R

Army Form C. 2118
Sheet 2

WAR DIARY
or
INTELLIGENCE SUMMARY.
(Erase heading not required.)

Place	Date	Hour	Summary of Events and Information	Remarks and references to Appendices
Dunkirk	16.4.19	At 07.45 hours the Battalion paraded, and marched down to the Docks. Embarkation was completed by 09.30 hours and at 09.45 hours, the Battalion sailed from France after 4 years and 8 months on active service. Strength of the Cadre on Embarkation was:- 4 officers 54 O.R. (*1 Officer was temporarily attached in Dunkirk on duty pending arrival of the Cadre at Preston this being later.)	

R.V. Berkeley Lt. Colonel
Comdg 1st Loyal N. Luna R

23.4.19